LETTING GO OF THE
GLITZ

The true story of one woman's struggle to live the simple life in Chelsea

*Dear Niche
much Love
Julia
X*

Julia
Stephenson

Julia Steph

♕

Crown House Publishing Ltd
www.crownhouse.co.uk

First published by
Crown House Publishing Ltd
Crown Buildings, Bancyfelin, Carmarthen,
Wales, SA33 5ND, UK
www.crownhouse.co.uk

British Library of Cataloguing-in-Publication Data
A catalogue entry for this book is available
from the British Library.

13-digit ISBN 978-184590142-4

Pages 33 and 222 extract from *Affluenza* by Oliver James,
published by Vermillion. Reprinted by kind permission of The
Random House Group Ltd.

Page 212 extract from *Bits of Me Are Falling Apart* by William Leith,
published by Bloomsbury. Reprinted with kind permission.

Disclaimer   This is a true account. However, some names,
identifying characteristics and time sequences have been changed
to protect the guilty.

Edited by Emma Tuck

To Steve

Acknowledgements

A CHAIN of good luck made this book possible.

First of all, thanks to *SHE* magazine which commissioned me to write an article about recycling, excitingly entitled 'She gave up the champagne lifestyle to go green' (I lied about giving up champagne of course — there are limits). Also thanks to GMTV, which on the back of this article filmed me dispensing string-saving tips at home. Somehow they talked my long-suffering inamorato, S, into peeing on our compost heap, replaying the footage twice (in case anyone missed it the first time) in front of six million viewers. One of those watching was my prospective publisher, Caroline Lenton, to whom I am eternally grateful, for she is the one who tracked me down and commissioned me to write this book. I am also hugely indebted to my endlessly patient and inspired editor, Emma Tuck, who tactfully steered things to their final conclusion. And of course thanks to S, who in the line of a Kate Bush song, makes me laugh and cry (and everything else in between) at the same time. It wouldn't have been half as much fun without you.

If the minds of living beings are impure, their land is also impure, but if their minds are pure, so is their land. There are not two lands, pure or impure in themselves. The difference lies solely in the good or evil of our minds.

Nichiren Daishonin

Every one of us can make a contribution. And quite often we are looking for the big things and forget that, wherever we are, we can make a contribution. ... Sometimes I tell myself, I may only be planting a tree here, but just imagine what's happening if there are billions of people out there doing something. Just imagine the power of what we can do.

Dr Wangari Maathai

Prologue

Now the recession has kicked in, I look back to the boom years and wonder, what were we thinking? For many years I, like so many others, was caught up in an extravagant consumer spiral — buying stuff I didn't need, stressing myself out by moving house every year in a constant attempt to trade up the property ladder (oh, the misery!) and taking long-distance holidays that left me more exhausted than if I'd stayed at home. I witnessed those around me working round the clock and falling apart to fund the extravagant, unaffordable lifestyle to which so many of us aspired.

With man-made climate instability the biggest threat facing us, it's timely that popular new movements are reflecting the thrifty *zeitgeist* without even needing to mention words like eco, green or sustainable. We have the mouth-watering Slow Food movement which promotes local food produced in rhythm with the seasons and fair pay for all those involved in the supply chain. Slow Travel eschews the misery of the modern airport and encourages us to enjoy travelling by train, ferry and foot, and to see the journey as part of the holiday.

Tom Hodgkinson similarly embraces the joys of slowing down in his politely revolutionary magazine *The Idler* which argues that idleness is eco-friendly and that to save the planet we need to relax and do less. Meanwhile, elusive groups such as the Cloud Appreciation Society and the Lying Around in Fields Society suggest that by being less driven we will be happier and save money in the process. It's a revolution in thinking — after years of being driven to achieve, to acquire, to shop till we dropped, the new wisdom is less is more. Hurrah!

Practising Buddhism for seventeen years has also changed my perspective. As Buddhist philosopher Dr Daisaku Ikeda explains: 'A barren, destructive mind produces a barren, devastated natural environment. The desertification of our planet is created by the desertification of the human spirit.'

Thus living a green life means we have to change from the inside first. Unless we transform our belief systems about what constitutes happiness we will go on grabbing and plundering what we can't afford until both we and the planet are extinguished.

This book is a description of my journey to reach these same conclusions through various incarnations — from sports car driving Stepford wife, married alive in the Surrey suburbs, wrestling with my hostess trolley and incompatible BMW-driving husband, to someone who, fifteen years down the line, is finally happy in her own skin and in a relationship I could only have dreamt of back then.

I took some strange detours along the way.

Attempts to cope with the fallout of my hideous divorce turned me into a frantic spiritual shopper and dolphin botherer *par extraordinaire*, trying to find happiness with feng shui, crystals, ruinously expensive Tony Robbins fire-walking courses and a trip to the Himalayas 'to find myself'. I ended up with a bright red apartment, a broken heart, burnt feet and dysentery — not to say a depleted bank account and enough carbon emissions to make me hang my head in shame.

Chakras still confused, I threw myself into the heady nineties and the ritzy life of an It-girl. Flashbulbs and champagne corks popped while aristocratic boyfriends came and went. On paper my life looked glamorous but inside I was often heartbroken, racing around chasing my tail, never feeling I fitted in. We live in a world where money, glitz, status and celebrity are seen as prerequisites for happiness but as those who have acquired these baubles of 'success' will attest they are no guarantee of contentment. A cliché but true. Sadly, many of us will have to learn through bitter experience that while material benefits are not to be sniffed at, the structure of your life must be sound before you can fully enjoy them.

Truly, I've served my time shopping, going to openings of envelopes, endlessly pursuing designer bags on eBay, enduring cultural events in an attempt to appear intellectual, falling in love with unsuitable Porsche-driving men and taking fancy holidays in the sun.

One day I woke up and realised I hate parties, shopping is tiring and boring, Birkin bags are impossibly heavy (and don't even fit over your shoulder so you can't keep your hands free), vacations in the sun mean enduring airport hell, and prematurely wrinkled skin and men in fast cars are compensating for inadequacies in other areas (see Chapter 12). Give me a man on a bike any day of the week.

Changing my values and living at a slower pace is a huge relief. Now I get my kicks from writing about the ups and downs of greening my life, fighting and losing elections on behalf of the Green Party and forcibly indoctrinating my long-suffering boyfriend S — a builder not a banker, thank goodness — into the joys of a green life.

He has taken to peeing on the compost heap (it speeds decomposition if you were wondering), making briquettes from old newspapers and chopping wood for our zero-emission wood-burning stove with some enthusiasm — but he still forgets to take off the tops of bottles before recycling (*sacre bleu!*), is yet to wear the cheery Kermit-green hemp boxer shorts foisted on him at Christmas, and retains an unhealthy attachment to a vile diesel-belching white van.

Sometimes, after a particularly enthusiastic lesson on the joys of greenery, his screams can be heard all over Chelsea, but he is sticking with it despite many lapses (as I write he is booking himself an all-you-can-eat-and-drink-for-£199 package holiday in Mexico), but he's a grown man, what can I do?

Chapter 1

The good life goes horribly wrong ...

I LIVE in a top floor flat in Chelsea, slap bang next to Peter Jones, department store and Mother Ship to all Sloanes within a six hundred mile radius, give or take the odd mile. I'm so close that sitting at my desk on my four foot by five foot patio writing this I'm eyeball to eyeball with the haberdashery department.

I live firmly in the urban jungle — not the easiest location you might think for someone wanting to live a simpler, greener life. But these days, living in a city is often far greener than living in a distant rural outpost. For starters I don't need a car, and buses and tubes are within easy striking distance. I can walk to local shops, there is a farmers' market around the corner at weekends and I have a farm box of authentically misshapen veg delivered every week.

But I did give the whole Good Life thing a go once. When I married in the 1990s, like thousands of other equally misguided townies, I went through a 'let's move to the country and grow our own vegetables' phase. The trouble is, my generation grew up watching *The Good Life* on telly and we thought self-sufficiency might be fun. I had also been much

taken during a visit to a country fair — unsuitably hosted in a
small piece of grubby parkland in Fulham — by the magical
but elusive organisation called the Lying Around in Fields
Society which proposes that we should all spend more time
lying around in fields instead of rushing around chasing our
tails. Their premise is that by lying around in fields you are
doing no harm whatsoever to the planet and you are doing
yourself a whole load of good by connecting yourself with
the earth and giving yourself time to reflect.

I thought this a marvellous idea but as a multi-tasking
townie I knew I'd never manage it: I'd end up taking along a
laptop, mobile phone, my teach-yourself-German textbooks
and quite possibly my 'how to make your own soya milk'
DVDs, and disturbing all the other lying around in fields
people. However, once I moved to the country I determined
to really throw myself into the whole field thing. I couldn't
wait to stop 'doing' and practise 'being' — yeahhh!

The trouble is, it is even noisier in the countryside now
than it is in London. Chainsaws, busy airports, roads and
the growth of ghastly leisure pursuits like paintballing,
clay pigeon shooting and off-road driving make rural life
an aural onslaught. Occasionally at Christmas some of the
headscarved ladies in Peter Jones might lose it a bit but that's
about as noisy as it gets in my urban eyrie.

But I didn't know this when I persuaded Paul, my then
husband, to exchange my cosy Fulham house where we were
very happy for a concrete house in the darkest depths of the
Sussex countryside. Here we would lie around romantically
in fields and, away from the city at last, have time to smell
the flowers.

I had vague dreams of recreating the Home Counties
tranquillity of childhood, before my father pushed off, my

mother went blonde and everything fell apart. In those distant days the only noise was from the occasional splash as Pimms-sodden guests crashed into the swimming pool.

No one talks much about feng shui any more, but it occurred to me that whilst Paul and I had been very happy in London, soon after moving to the concrete house things unravelled quickly. It may seem superstitious blaming a house for one's circumstances but there's no denying the place had a bad atmosphere.

Many people are seduced by the dream of living in a house with no near neighbours, but this is a mistake. Humans are pack animals and don't thrive in isolation. In a stroke we exchanged a tube station and two bus routes on our doorstep for zero public transport. In London I rarely used my car, as everything was within walking distance, but Haslemere was another story — buying a pint of milk or a newspaper meant a six-mile round trip.

In the 1990s there was no organic food to be had for miles but this didn't bother me as I was going to grow my own scrumptious biodynamic vegetables from seed. Miserably my dreams of self-sufficiency soon fell on stony ground as the poor soil yielded nothing but weeds.

People complain of misspent youth in bars and nightclubs, but my early twenties were squandered slaving over wheelbarrows of stinking pig manure desperately trying to coax growth from the barren ground. Whilst I'd been the one envied by single girlfriends for fulfilling the Bridget Jones dream — getting hitched and moving to the country to live in rustic bliss — the tables soon turned and I was the one envying them. I was knee-deep in Aga catalogues, making jam that never set, trying to play golf and other hideous suburban pursuits that I followed with dogged determination. I was hopeless at all of them, and while Paul's star rose — reaching dizzy heights in the accounting profession as well as becoming the lynchpin of the Liphook Golf Club — I grew increasingly depressed. I had no time to lie around around in fields and I had no time to smell the flowers, either as I was too busy with my domestic responsibilities.

To be fair, my Martha Stewart aspirations were entirely self-imposed. Paul wasn't the one demanding that I bake my own bread or shine the wooden floors with an ancient 1930s floor polisher using homemade beeswax polish. I had been infected by Martha madness and it was exhausting. It irritated me that Paul had embraced country life with gusto. He was good at chopping down trees, driving around the steep, narrow lanes and even enjoyed the long, pointless country walks that drove me mad with boredom. He was even good at relaxing — something I couldn't get the hang of at all.

How I longed to give it all up and step into my city friends' Jimmy Choos. I wanted to be wined and dined by glossy Italian bankers and whisked off to exciting European cities by them. I dreamt of escaping the demands of the unwieldy concrete house, its huge barren garden and, most of all, Paul and his great band of golfing cronies who descended like starving locusts every weekend. I realised I'd rather boil my own head than face another interminable weekend wheeling out my matching avocado bowls and gleaming hostess trolley.

I would spend days preparing for these feasts. Many people think that the Galloping Gourmet — the cookery writer famous for his extravagant creamy cooking — is dead, but let me tell you, his candle still burns brightly in this distant outpost of the Surrey suburbs.

The efforts I went to! I made bread, cakes and yogurt.

I even baked my own wholemeal croissants, encrusted with organic toasted sesame seeds. I foraged in the garden and local woods for wild food. Foraging is fashionable now, but in the early nineties was unheard of. No wonder my nettle and nutmeg soufflés, which I had cunningly passed off as spinach, caused panic in my guests while my chickweed rissoles were the talk of Haslemere, but not in a good way. I realised regretfully that my lean green cuisine was just too outré for the Home Counties.

In a rare trip to London to visit Peter Jones (their range of organic cleaning fluids was far more comprehensive than anything I could find in Haslemere), I gazed up at the sooty city skyline, fantasising about living in a rooftop eyrie (like the one I live in now — this story *does* have a happy ending) quite alone and unconstricted by Stepford Wife constraints. But I didn't have the courage to leave. Muddled and not knowing which way to turn, should I stay or should I go, I consulted a psychiatrist at the Priory who was kind and sympathetic: 'If you don't know what to do, do nothing.' Wise counsel.

I didn't know what to do so I stayed put. The psychiatrist also said that I'd know when to leave because I wouldn't be able to face having sex with Paul any more. At the time, like most married women, I did what I could to put it off for as long as possible but I could still just about manage once a week — if I gritted my teeth. It seemed a bit mean not to when he was so keen and it stopped me feeling guilty for being so horrible to him.

But, sensing something was wrong, he had begun suggesting we 'try for a baby'. Until then we had relied on condoms but fearing he might sabotage them I'd invested in an organic honey cap — honey being an exceptionally powerful spermicide — and tried to put him off wherever possible.

I splashed out on an unappetising selection of heavy flame-resistant hemp nightgowns I had spotted in an organic catalogue, reasoning that if they were sturdy enough to resist fire perhaps they would repel husbands too. Indeed the fabric was so unyielding that on several occasions trying to remove it had proved such hard work that we had both given up and gone to sleep.

But I did start to hatch an escape route with new interests that Paul didn't share. I joined the local Friends of the Earth group and began attending meetings in the musty village hall. Being green wasn't the glamorous occupation of fashionistas and movie stars that it is today. No, back then the clichés were all true and our hempy group was as beardy, sandal-clad and resolutely gluten-free as it's possible to get. But I liked them all, and had finally found a tribe that I had more in common with than the grisly materialistic golfers and bankers that made up our usual social circle.

Thus emboldened I joined a writing class to vent my suburban spleen. There, alongside a vast number of similarly bored housewives, their expensive Mont Blanc pens (gifts from their exhausted Goldman Sachs husbands) speeding across the page, we would compose terrible poems about our inner turmoil.

I began an autobiographical novel and, to Paul's chagrin, worked feverishly on it day and night. The compost heap suffered similar neglect and refused to decompose, leaving a terrible stench and blot on the landscape. The neighbours were incandescent.

Desperately miserable I began a doomed misalliance with an unemployed vegan drummer I met in the local health food shop. Skulking around Haslemere engaged in adulterous pursuits provided inspiration for my tales of marital misery. I saw myself as a modern Madame Bovary and began quoting chunks of the novel at my bemused husband. If I'm honest I found Flaubert as impenetrable as he did, but it did at least inspire me to persevere with my own bored housewife novel which was now well underway.

My writing schedule was intense, so domestic standards slipped, dust gathered and cobwebs appeared. The vacuum broke and I never got round to mending it. The healthy home-cooked meals were replaced by takeaways from the notorious but convenient Haslemere-Hot-Dogz. When it was closed down by an environmental health officer, I fed Paul on frozen TV dinners from FreezaWorld and the fridge soon toppled with arctic rolls, oven chips and raspberry ripple ice cream. My green dreams had collapsed in smithereens — for now at least.

One day, faced with the ghastly realisation that the face on the pillow next to me would stay the same till one of us died, I packed my bags and bolted to the fleshpots of Knightsbridge.

On my own at last, having disentangled myself from the clutches of the musician who was becoming increasingly possessive, I went blonde with relief and, without gainful employment, embarked on an intensive self-help odyssey. During divorce some people turn to drink and drugs but these were of no interest to me. My crutch was spiritual shopping — Princess Diana had nothing on me. No numerologist, shaman, soothsayer, dowser or astrologer (Ayurvedic or Western) was safe from my call. Bells were bonged, whale music murmured, feng shui consultants shuffled in and out bearing wind chimes and crystals and my bookshelves heaved with self-help tomes. I embraced a macrobiotic diet, travelled to Nantucket and Ireland to consult psychics, one of whom insisted I must visit the Himalayas which would enable me to find the true peace and happiness I was seeking.

This suggestion couldn't have come at a better time. I was desperate to escape London and a sexual obsession with a heartless but devastatingly handsome German banker called Holst. He was tall, blond and wore crisp cornflower blue shirts that matched his cold cobalt eyes — I'm sure this was intentional. He would torture me with late night phone calls during which he would discuss existentialism while playing 'Riders on the Storm' softly in the background — I'm convinced he timed the ebbs and flows of our mean- ingful conversations with the crashing of waves in the song. Whoosh, crash, trickle, whoosh, whoosh ... It was all very sexy and phallic, cunning bastard, but the cruel thing was he'd talk about sex all the time but had decided our rela- tionship should remain celibate, as I was still married. This was maddeningly true because the decree nisi still hadn't come through and Paul was always coming round to pick up stuff. After years of making excuses to get out of sex, it was a cruel irony to have the tables turned on me by the tantalis- ing Teuton, but no more than I deserved.

Soon after my consultation with the Nantucket psychic I booked myself onto a flight to Nepal, impulsively pitch- ing up at Kathmandu airport with nowhere to stay. This was an oversight as the place was teeming with shifty look- ing hawkers and tuk-tuk drivers. Clutching my *Lonely Planet* guidebook I ignored the hustlers and took a cab to the rec- ommended Kathmandu Inn, reputedly a haven for weary, besieged Europeans. It sounded perfect; however, it was a dark, dank and dismal place, full of ancient libidinous hippies strumming tuneless guitars and smoking pot. After one night I escaped to the countryside and spent a further two weeks travelling round this chaotic, exasperating and beautiful country which had absolutely bewitched me. As the days rolled by I became aware that the anxieties of the past and my fears of the future were falling away, leaving me feeling happy and excited. I barely thought about Holst, except to wonder why on earth I'd been so keen.

Returning to Kathmandu I checked into a glorious airy colonial hotel and began chatting to one of the receptionists, Naju, a slightly built Nepali with sparkling dark eyes and a quick sense of humour. We immediately hit it off and, despite strict hotel rules forbidding fraternisation with the guests, embarked on a secretive and romantic affair, made all the more bittersweet because I only had a week before returning home. On our first evening together we hired (rather I did — he had no money) a tuk-tuk to visit Swayambhunath Stupa, an ancient, magical temple bathed in moonlight and teeming with pilgrims, families and wild monkeys swinging and swooping around us. Candles flickered in the darkness and devout Buddhists spun prayer wheels and kneeled inside a number of small chapels that made up the temple. The air was heavy with burning incense, the chatter of monkeys and the endless murmuring of prayers. It was also crowded, grubby and noisy, all the things I usually abhor, but something in the spirit of the place swept me along with it.

But by the end of the week the romance, which had started off so promisingly, was going downhill fast. As I got ripped off every time I tried to buy something I'd quickly realised that it was much easier for Naju to take care of the paltry amounts needed to buy drinks and pay for tuk-tuks, so

I handed him my purse. Within a few days he took it upon himself to start distributing its contents to the many beggars that thronged our path — maddeningly he dished out my small change with the superior and benevolent air of a mini pasha. The following day when he took me to the airport I realised on checking in that due to 'his' largesse I had no money left to pay the airport tax. Grrr!

But all thoughts of the grasping Naju soon left me as the plane took off and tears streamed down my cheeks. A sensible Nepalese steward dispensed tissues and sat down on the armrest to chat. 'Are you missing someone?' he asked, noting I was travelling alone. I glanced out of the window catching a final glimpse of the glorious Himalayas as they faded from view. I knew that my love affair had been with a country, not a man, but the ache in my heart was like leaving a lover all the same.

'You may leave Nepal,' he said, 'but Nepal will never leave you.' I knew exactly what he meant. My visit had been utterly extraordinary and I wondered if I would ever experience anything quite like it again.

I would never forget the mountains, the temples, the chaos, the spirit of the country. And contrarily, despite my misty eyes, I felt incredibly irritated about Naju. Imagine, he had left me with no Nepalese money for the airport. The cheek of it! However, despite all this, he had brought a magical quality to my trip. By introducing me to his friends and taking me to places I would never have visited alone he had shown me a glimpse of the country that otherwise would have remained hidden to me.

Soon after my return I was lying on my bed feeling misty eyed about the trip when the phone rang. It was a Nepalese operator asking if I would accept a reverse charge call from

Naju. 'Most certainly not!' I replied and slammed down the receiver.

But Naju was tenacious. Emails and phone calls followed. 'Do not forget your poor brother in Nepal,' he pleaded. 'Please sponsor me. I want to come to London and live with you!'

'Oh do get a grip!' I replied tersely, 'I've got quite enough brothers as it is' (due to my parents' various marriages this is indeed true), but my irritation seemed lost on him. 'You must stop contacting me. I'm getting married' I lied firmly, 'and my fiancé insists you stop!'

This did the trick and I never heard from him again. But in time my irritation faded. That's Nepal — maddening, awful and wonderful, all at the same time.

Chapter 2

Spiritual shopping can damage your wealth

I HADN'T been home very long when I was soon knee-deep in tantalising self-help catalogues. Although I was deeply tempted by the Landmark Forum and the Hoffman Process I was put off by having to share small carpeted bedrooms with strangers — for the prices they were charging 'patients' should get a luxurious bedroom, v-spring mattress and marble bathroom full of delicious unguents at the very least.

But caution flew out of the window after listening to a Tony Robbins CD called *Awaken the Giant Within* and I impulsively signed up for a round-the-world self-help extravaganza starting with fire walking in Frankfurt. Tony Robbins has been enormously successful — his books and DVDs sell in their millions and he attracts a huge following at his courses.

The brochure promised that the course would 'vanquish everything that may be holding you back from utilising the force that can instantly change your life' and that I would learn to 'instantly place yourself in peak emotional, mental and physical states and achieve results beyond your wildest dreams!'

Truly, how could any spiritual shopper resist? Could you?

But if I'd known what a nightmare it was all going to be I'd have stayed at home.

The following weekend I arrived in Frankfurt and with great trepidation crept into the enormous city auditorium, jam-packed with four thousand jostling, flag-waving Germans. As Tony swung confidently towards the stage on a rope he got stuck and was left swinging for several terrifying minutes. Members of his entourage dashed onto the stage and deposited him gingerly on the ground, from where he immediately began to boost us with positive life strategies. As he warbled on late into the night I got chatting to the chap next to me. He was called Hans and we immediately bonded through boredom — everyone was getting so much out of Tony's *bon mots*, but like the emperor with no clothes, we just didn't get it at all.

Eventually Tony ran out of steam, groovy music blared and we were encouraged to dance and hug as many people as possible. This turned into a sort of mass grope, sexual confidence being a core part of the Tony ethos. I couldn't face it. The Germans invented the naked mixed sauna experience so they really get into this sort of thing — at similar courses in the UK everyone just shakes hands — so I stayed with Hans and snogged him instead. Not for long though — next up was the dreaded fire walking.

Fires had been lit, tribal music throbbed. Drums pounded and adrenaline surged through our terrified veins as we stood in line waiting for our turn to run over the red-hot burning coals. Terror had engendered a primal wartime lust in the participants, many of whom were locked in steamy embraces. Indeed, Hans and I had become so bored and disillusioned with the whole thing we were now similarly enmeshed. Unfortunately this meant we missed some of the pep talk teaching us how to 'get in state' by chanting 'cool moss, cool moss' (a physiological ploy to cool us down) as we ran over the sizzling coals. We did try this but we still ended up burning our feet.

As we had our feet bandaged later, along with hundreds of other positive thinking failures, I was downcast but quickly revived when Hans suggested he'd 'had enough of this bollocks' (his English was impressive) and did I want to come with him to the South of France where he was doing some business.

We spent a fairly chaste night at our respective hotels and the next morning he picked me up in his Vorsprung durch Technik Audi with its self-warming seats and air con. We were both dizzy with relief at escaping the day's challenges which included jumping off a one hundred-foot telegraph pole 'to conquer our fear of life'.

We enjoyed an epic drive through Germany, stopping off at a luxurious chateau for the night. But a shadow soon clouded our thrilling escape when the following morning his suitcase spilled open and all the towels from our hotel bathroom fell out.

I was dumbfounded — did he have no towels at home? A pall descended on our journey. At the next service station his credit card was refused. I'd assumed he was comfortably off but he admitted business was not going so well. But I found him hugely attractive so I put the towels and imminent penury out of my mind.

On the outskirts of Cannes we stopped at a service station for a snack where my bag, containing my credit card, passport, diary and phone, was snatched. I was devastated. Disconsolately we made our way to a hotel run by a friend of his, the authoress of several conspiracy theory novels. It was dark, freezing and pouring with rain when we arrived. Hans was in a foul mood and there was an unspoken feeling that my bag theft was karmic retribution for his towel thieving. The hotelier/conspiracy theorist, a dour, paranoid German woman who had some kind of crush on Hans, wasn't happy to see me at all. Utterly exhausted we had a blistering row during which he accused me of being a spoiled rich girl who would only stay in luxury hotels and who had no conception of the real world.

'Tell me something I don't know!' I scowled. 'At least I don't go round pinching towels!' My outburst was so violent I couldn't help noticing that the MDF walls juddered quite noticeably.

Hans stomped off to discuss the latest political plots with our hostess, whilst I tossed and turned in the cold hard bed. Neither of us slept a wink. The following morning we arranged for him to drop me back at the station. I was longing to return to London but was ridiculously disappointed when he agreed so readily to my departure. Strangely enough, I'd become quite keen on him again. Anyway, we both apologised and bid a teary farewell but I never heard from him again.

Before all this I'd been feeling quite cheerful, what with the new flat and the relief of being separated from Paul, but the whole Tony Robbins debacle had sunk me into a terrible gloom. I was so depressed my doctor prescribed Prozac, but in a triumph of hope over experience I decided to go on another Tony Robbins course — this time in Fiji. I'd paid for all the trips up front so I thought I may as well get on with it — and surely Tony's positive life strategies would kick in for me soon?

Before I left I remember traipsing round the shops with my mother, too depressed to speak. She'd had a low impression of Hans ever since I'd confessed the towel pinching episode. 'At least he'll have plenty of towels to bag his space by the swimming pool on his next summer holiday,' she sniffed. The thought of Hans and the rest of his country folk energetically rising at 6 a.m. to bag the best sunloungers in the Canaries and other Teutonic hotspots with their stolen towels was indeed deeply unappealing.

I could have saved my carbon emissions and stayed at home, for Fiji was no more successful than fire walking in Germany. I had expected that everyone would be staying at the luxurious Fijian resort owned by Tony Robbins, where the course was being held, but to my horror some sort of bizarre singleton apartheid was in operation and the single participants were bussed out every night while the couples stayed put in the sumptuous resort.

When I complained I was told that the selection for who slept where was random and that I had just 'got unlucky'. Apparently it was to do with my 'karma'. Huh, as if! My karma regarding luxurious accommodation had always been tip-top until now — what were they on about?

The singletons' lodgings were a mosquito-infested swampy hotel forty minutes away and I found myself sharing with a beautiful but nutty American heiress who became increasingly deranged as the week went on. Every night she tried to get into my bed but she wasn't exclusive in her favours and quickly developed a crush on Robbins, regularly throwing herself onto the stage during his monologues. The fire walking soon sent her right over the top and she threatened suicide which resulted in the Fijian National Guard having to stand sentry outside our room to stop her drowning herself. Eventually she was sedated and carted back to LA.

Although I could see that Robbins had integrity and I was impressed by his 'can do' ethos, his energy and the way he inspired those around him, his courses left me feeling strangely depressed. I realised I would have gained far more by just reading his boosting books and watching his inspirational DVDs in the comfort of my own home.

Ironically, on all the courses I attended, despite the fact that we were apparently being trained to be 'leaders', any sort of independent thought was firmly suppressed and there seemed an unhealthy focus on consumerism and money. This was symbolised by the Platinum Club. At this time it cost about US$30,000 to join and enabled the lucky member to wear a tacky platinum-coloured medallion and share meals with Tony (quite honestly, once you'd witnessed his table manners you'd pay US$30,000 *not* to dine with him).

The lucky medallion men were terribly libidinous and confident in their right to exercise *droit de seigneur* with any girl who took their fancy. Stomping around, clanging their tiny gongs, many of the girls thought they were quite a catch. During one endless seminar Robbins encouraged us to join up by outlining the amazing boundless pleasures that awaited those who could afford the fee. The Platinum website is packed with glossy, grinning people in mouth-watering locations — they frolic on camels in deserts, swim through waterfalls and are pictured boarding private jets. The site gushes 'the world is our playground' (Grrr! I wanted to shout at these grinning gas-guzzlers that the world is *not* our playground to trash at will!). During one of our lectures Robbins described escorting some members to a top night-club in Paris where the doorman had chucked a group off their table so that the superior Platinum gang could sit in comfort. What sort of person does this appeal to?

If this wasn't bad enough I had to endure endless seminars during which we were kept hydrated with bottles of 'oxygenated' Penta water (a ludicrously over-hyped water air-freighted from California) and endless bottles of the apparently silica-rich Fijian water — in the same bottles you see in Waitrose. Water was poured from these plastic bottles into plastic cups which we drank out of once, before they were thrown away in vast plastic bin bags.

I spent a disagreeable week jumping into rivers full of poisonous fish to learn to 'trust the universe' and listening to the Platinum guys rave about 'swimming with Tony', like he was some sort of magic dolphin. But all the time I was tormented by the hideous thought that we were poisoning Fijian landfill sites with festering plastic bottles and cups that were going to take up to a thousand years to degrade.

Tentative suggestions that we keep our cups with us to be refilled were met with incredulous looks by our 'trainer', a brainwashed Robbins apprentice who was trying to keep our team in order.

I hoped to be distracted from our growing waste mountain when Stormin' Norman, the Gulf War veteran, jetted in to give us a pep talk. Strutting onto the stage, squeezed into a pair of tight black jeans (perhaps he was as waterlogged as we were) accompanied by thrilling *Top Gun*-style footage of swooping planes, he waited to take questions from the adoring audience.

'If Kuwait had exported potatoes not oil would we have invaded?' I piped up from the back. Unsatisfied by his waffle about human rights in Kuwait I went for my Richard Gear moment, 'But what about Tibet — the human rights abuses there are far worse!' before being arm-wrestled to my seat by my trainer and force-fed a bottle of Fijian water: 'Honey you need to rehydrate!'

It was downhill from there really. So don't get me started on Fiji (overrated mosquito-ridden place — no letters please) or its water. Save yourself some air miles and leave Fijian water for the Fijians. They need all the silica they can get.

Chapter 3

Help, I've become an 'It-girl'!

SOMETIMES I look back and think of all the stress, money and carbon emissions I could have saved by avoiding these disagreeable spiritual shopping trips but it's easy to be wise in retrospect. Besides, several friends and acquaintances whiled away their twenties in a fog of alcohol and drugs — necessitating expensive and usually unsuccessful trips to rehab facilities — so I wasn't the only one wasting my money, and at least I did see a bit of the world.

My trip to Fiji had been so disagreeable that when I got home I couldn't face any more spiritual shopping. With my decree nisi at last complete, I threw myself into the London whirl. I was soon introduced to Piers, an eligible marquess; we hit it off and started dating.

Piers was a generous host and was always having parties at his palatial Kensington home. People came to stay and sometimes never left — there was a flat at the top of the house stuffed with party animals who lived on canapés and champagne and remained in permanent situ for years. One such was Moshe, a hulking Israeli ex-soldier now businessman. He was handsome but unbelievably hirsute — he had hair all over his back like a gorilla. Nonetheless he had great success with the ladies and managed to seduce one a week, on average, whilst in London.

He wasn't that fussy — they just had to be blonde and he was happy enough. He prided himself on his international 'man of mystery' allure and would never say what he did. If you asked he'd mumble 'import–export' and then wrestle you onto the nearest chaise longue for a spot of rumpy pumpy. Despite being one of Piers's closest friends he was always chasing me round the house and telling me fibs about his part in the Entebbe Raid in a desperate attempt to get me into bed. He was only 9 years old in 1976, but this didn't stop him from convincing everyone he'd played a small but crucial role in the entire operation.

Moshe was the perfect foil to Piers who was the absolute gentleman and would as soon arm wrestle me onto a chaise longue than do handstands in the street. Contrarily, while Piers preferred to talk rather than have sex, Moshe never wanted to talk, he just wanted to have sex. It was amazing how two such different souls could coexist so happily in the same house.

I had a wonderful year with Piers. If he wasn't having a party we'd be invited to one of his friends' houses who was. He introduced me to his aristocratic relatives and wooed me during huntin', shootin' and fishin' weekends at their grand country piles. The smarty set have been very cunning and have cleverly fostered an image of penury in the media to avoid envy and higher taxes. When we hear about toffs they are usually gloomily surveying their run-down castles and carrying buckets to catch the drips from their enormous lead roofs which they can't afford to mend. So it came as a bit of a surprise to me, a solidly middle class girl from Guildford, to discover the reams of aristos that still live in great style below the parapet of public attention. Admittedly, the ones I met were all very much north of Watford, living in astonishingly feudal splendour, kings of all they surveyed.

It was fascinating observing all this from an outsider's point of view, and it was fun for a bit, but so much of this world is based on money and status, not wit and character. Having a title provides unquestioned entrée into the smartest circles but grand soirées are no guarantee of sparkling conversation. Indeed, at the turreted castle of a foppish baronet all the men wanted to talk about was interior decor. The lack of testosterone at many upper class gatherings is so alarming one wonders how they breed at all.

While I was trying to rev up Piers, fend off Moshe and experience the high life, the gossip columns picked up on me and I endured a brief flourishing as an 'It-girl'.

Today, in the socially responsible, downsizing noughties, we look down on the term It-girl but in the aspirational 1990s 'it' was a byword for glamour, money, glitz, good looks and social cachet. The stock market was booming and London hummed, fuelled by fat cat City bonuses and excesses. Greed was good; flash (and flesh) was fab.

Princess Diana was in her prime and a slew of young Sloane Rangers swept along in her wake. In the past they would probably have been debs, but in the egalitarian 1990s they had been rebranded as It-girls and I had the right credentials (if one didn't look too closely) to join their throng.

I was now appearing frequently in the gossip columns so it was a great time to publish my first novel, *Pandora's Diamond*, as the publicity would be assured. My publishers decided that my Unique Selling Point was the 'It-girl writes novel' angle — after all, nobody thought an It-girl could read, let alone write. It was an extraordinary concept for the time. It was quickly dubbed 'the It-girl's bible', even though it was actually about my miserable marital experiences, but whatever ...

However, there was a deluge of bored housewife novels that year, and I was desperate to promote mine. Fearing the book I had poured my heart and soul into would sink into oblivion without the oxygen of publicity, I did a deal with the devil and attracted the exposure my family detested. To guarantee maximum 'puff' I employed the legendary It-person's favourite PR agency, Schmooze Associates, to organise the book launch to end all book launches.

Schmooze were very successful, judging by the amount of coverage their posh protégés, including Tara Palmer-Tomkinson, achieved for attending parties, shopping and, well, that was about it. Petronella, the doyenne of Schmooze, was happy to take me on. She was thrilled with my family connections and that I was dating a handsome, eligible marquess with his own stately home in the centre of London. Very soon my fax machine was whirring with invitations. I was interviewed in glossy magazines and newspapers, and photographed 'sharing a joke' with many well known It-people of the era, whose names are now sadly forgotten.

My book launch was a dazzling success, attracting reams of publicity in the society mags and newspapers. Piers had offered to hold it at his plush pad and the party pulsated with the cream of cafe society. Henry and Lily Brocklehurst, Beverley Bloom and her brother 'Baron' — who made a startling entrance in a bright yellow Aston Martin and even Steve Norris, the Tory MP, had suddenly appeared, having apparently drifted in on hearing the siren call of revelry from the street below. Celebrity yoga teachers, gossip columnists, hairdressers, breakfast TV presenters and personal make-up artists made up the rest of the gathering.

It was a glittering throng and Petronella purrrred with pleasure.

All that glisters is not gold, and indeed the reality was a lot less glittering than it looked. I only knew about a quarter of the people there, but propelled on pink champagne and bonhomie I smiled and tried to make conversation with people I didn't know, who didn't know me and that I would never see again. They had no interest in books; they were there because their publicists had told them to go, the champagne was free, the canapés were fabulous, plus it was being held in the private home of one of the country's premier aristocrats and would be reported in all the glossies.

Halfway through the party, Tara Palmer-Tomkinson materialised, glamorous and assured in a slinky chocolate-coloured slip. Petronella anxiously propelled us together to get the all-important photo op that would guarantee coverage in next day's papers. I bared my teeth nervously and clutched my novel to ensure that it was photographed at a flattering angle. My attempts at sisterly solidarity with Tara fell on deaf ears and I was left wittering away to myself. Meanwhile, the flashbulbs popped and my smile grew tighter and more stretched. To my eternal shame I was too busy to talk to my mother, the one person who had actually read my novel, even poring over it for weeks to check for spelling mistakes. She confided later that she had left the party in tears.

My tenuous relationship with my family deteriorated even further after that night. One member, a struggling unpublished writer and conceptual artist, refused to speak to me for years afterwards. A hitherto close friend, who had been trying to get her own novel published for years, had taken me aside and whispered with feigned concern that 'some of our closest friends are saying you only got your book published because of your family connections'. A rabidly left-wing friend had a blazing row with Steve Norris about the wickedness of car ownership and road haulage before storming off on her bicycle. They say you discover who your friends are when times are tough, but it's truer to say that you know who your true friends are when you are successful — success can drive some people quite mad with envy. 'Why her?' they seethe, 'Why not me?'

Still the merry-go-round went on. But I was getting bored with the constant round of promotional parties that fuel this bright, shiny, luxury-product fuelled world. This isn't *real* society which abhors the glare of publicity. Piers loathed cafe society and I began to ignore many of the invitations to shampoo launches and shop openings that Schmooze insisted I attend.

But Petronella was intimidating and when she found out that I was slacking was absolutely livid: 'Tara manages to attend ten parties a night!' she would scream, 'What's WRONG with you!'

Tara had the pick of the invitations. If she couldn't go to a photo shoot or interview, Petronella would try to send me along instead, talking me up desperately to the client who most of the time wouldn't have a clue who I was. It was pulverising. If there was a league table of It-girls, I was definitely Woking FC to Tara's Manchester United.

Although Petronella was terrifying she had got me heaps of publicity for my novel, which was attracting great sales. I was delighted; my publisher was happy and eager for me to finish my second. Unfortunately the publicity focused much more on my reclusive family than my novel. The fact that I was a vegetarian and patron of Viva!, the radical animal rights charity, and a member of the Vestey family, whose fortune was largely based on the Dewhurst butcher empire, was too irresistible to ignore. I longed to talk about my novel but the focus was always on my family. How lovely it would be, I thought, to be known for myself, not my rellos for once. But this isn't the way the world works.

Senior family members loathed the attention. When I appeared in *Tatler* completely starkers, wearing nothing but a painted-on butcher's apron to promote my vegetarian beliefs, they hit the roof.

Now I realise that any success that causes a breakdown in family relations is simply not worth having. But back then, desperate for attention to feed my lack of confidence, I lost sight of what was important. If this wasn't bad enough, matters really came to a head when the curse of *Hello!* struck.

Petronella had palpitated in delight when she secured a glossy six-page spread with Piers 'at home' (at home at Piers's plush pad, not the tiny, grey, serviced apartment I was inhabiting at this time, I hasten to add). Unfortunately, Piers refused point-blank to be photographed. The deal hinged on his inclusion and Petronella went ballistic when I explained his horror of publicity.

Luckily the *Hello!* shoot duly went ahead without him. Piers was indeed cunningly caught in several photographs — a fleeting blurred figure in the background. Fortunately, as he never read *Hello!*, he never found out.

And then the curse struck …

An interview I'd done to promote my novel had incensed my father and, as a result, we did not speak for three years. A distant cousin that I had never met had dashed off a furious letter complaining (completely erroneously) at her portrayal in my novel as a cleaner, several others telephoned to complain that being featured in the magazine was 'the final straw' and that I was 'bringing the family into disrepute'.

Another had rung to complain that my book was 'shite' and refused to be in the same room as me, which led to me being excluded from family occasions for years afterwards.

I was so shocked by all of this I caught bronchitis which nearly turned into pneumonia. Madly, I refused to take the medicine I so desperately needed, instead seeking cures from various dubious faith healers. One evening I collapsed while staggering around Crouch End trying to find a healer but she just made me feel even worse. Eventually I saw sense and visited my family doctor who immediately prescribed antibiotics. I'm no fan of pill-popping, and will always seek out natural remedies as a first port of call, but without those tablets I think I would have died.

It took months to recover from the bronchitis, but as soon as I felt better I escaped to Switzerland to write my second novel, *Chalet Tiara*, inspired by the thrills — but mainly spills — of the It-girl jungle.

I have since worked hard to mend bridges with my family and we now enjoy an improved relationship. But when you are insecure and lack confidence, publicity becomes a drug, an addiction, reassuring you of your place in the world, even of your very existence. This hunger and need is common to many in the public eye; they seek fame to fill some deep void in their lives but however much attention they receive it's never enough to fill it. How I envied the elegant and low key who seek approval from no one but themselves!

Meanwhile the world becomes increasingly celebrity obsessed, with many people desperate to achieve the fifteen minutes of fame that they believe will solve all their problems. At the same time we are bombarded with suggestions that the more materially successful we are the happier we will be.

In his book *Affluenza*, psychologist Oliver James suggests

that many of us in the West are suffering from the 'afflu-enza virus'. He explains that sufferers 'place a high value on acquiring money and possessions, looking good in the eyes of others and wanting to be famous'.

'The great majority of people in English-speaking nations', he writes, 'now define their lives through earnings, posses-sions, appearances and celebrity, and those things are mak-ing them miserable because they impede the meeting of our fundamental needs.'

It is hard to avoid getting sucked into this modern epi-demic when confronted by glossy magazines full of celebri-ties at glitzy parties, but the reality behind those air-brushed pictures and wide collagen-enhanced smiles is not what it seems. I look back to my photographs of that time and though I looked glamorous and happy, I often felt lost, lonely and insecure. Years later I bumped into an acquaintance, a self-styled Italian prince, who had come to my book launch.

'That night you looked like a princess with the world at your feet!' he gushed. 'Your wonderful family, aristocratic boyfriend, the designer dress, all your glamorous society friends — and you'd just published a novel ... you were the girl with everything ... oh, how we all envied you!'

His face fell when I explained that it was all an illusion, a mere fairytale. I didn't dare tell him my dress was from Kookai — he might have had a complete breakdown.

But like many affluenza sufferers he was convinced that having the baubles was a guarantee of happiness. To a greater or lesser extent we are all victims of the epidemic, running round in circles, wearing ourselves out with our busy lives that look great from the outside while feeling shitty inside. I remembered the Lying Around in Fields Society and although I admired the concept I felt there was no way some-one like me, with my hunger to 'get on', would have time to lie around anywhere. I liked the idea of having time to smell the flowers, but … I didn't have time! Well, do you? And who were the Lying Around in Fields Society anyway? They didn't even have a website for goodness' sake! Of course, now I realise it takes a lot of effort to create a website and this sort of feverish promotion is just what they are trying to avoid.

But part of me knew it was time to radically change the way I thought and the way I lived. All my spiritual shopping had been interesting but hadn't actually made me feel any happier or significantly increased my understanding of what made the world tick. So when a friend invited me to a Buddhist meeting round the corner I decided to go along and find out more.

In the West, Buddhism is often seen as a form of spiritual shopping with core concepts, such as karma, meaninglessly banded around by people who don't know what they actually mean. But Buddhism is one of the world's oldest religions and is practised in different forms by millions of people worldwide. Maybe a bona fide religion would provide a more substantial and meaningful view of life that all my spiritual shopping had not.

Chapter 4

You don't have to shave your head to become a Buddhist

I WENT along to my first Buddhist meeting with some trepidation not knowing what to expect. Like most British people my knowledge of Buddhism was confined to visiting Buddhist temples in the Far East and I had a vague idea that real Buddhists wore orange robes, shaved their heads and meditated in caves and mountains. However, the meeting I went along to was held by a member of Soka Gakkai International, a form of lay Buddhism that originated in Japan and which is now one of the world's fastest growing religions, numbering over twelve million members.

At that first meeting I was told that when you purify yourself you will in turn purify your environment. It is a very empowering philosophy because instead of thinking, I'll be happy when this person changes or when I achieve this, it is up to us to change first and this will correspondingly create a change in others.

The Buddhist philosopher, Dr Daisaku Ikeda, president of Soka Gakkai International and recipient of the United Nations Peace Award and countless honorary doctorates and awards, explains that the quickest way for society to improve is for individuals improve themselves first:

Without surmounting the fundamental human delusions of greed, anger, and foolishness, we will not be able to solve the many problems that the world faces today, including the pre-occupation with economic growth, politics that are devoid of humanism, international conflicts, warfare, growing disparity between rich and poor, and rampant discrimination. ... the only real solution is for human beings themselves to change, that the sole key lies in 'human revolution'.

Members of SGI believe the key to elevating one's life-condition and creating a happier society is through chanting the phrase *Nam-myoho-renge-kyo*, the title of the Lotus Sutra. It purifies your life on the deepest possible level, allowing you to change established thought and behaviour patterns and see the world through fresh eyes.

It sounded pretty good to me, so I decided to give it a go. The chanting sounded quite strange at first but I persevered and chanted every day, desperate to see the changes in my life that were promised if I kept it up. Gradually I began to see differences — I became less needy, less selfish and much happier.

My life began to change quickly. Amicably splitting up from the very tolerant Piers — he could put up with the chanting, even me tipping a bowl of strawberries over a guest's head for wearing a fur coat at one of his parties, but the endless string of protests, rallies, actions and disappearing for weeks to Switzerland and Nantucket to plot my next novel meant I rarely saw him. Men thrive on propinquity, which is why they so often end up with their secretaries, housekeepers, cleaners and nannies. Unlike women who can pine for years over an unsuitable ex-boyfriend who has emigrated to Australia or the moon, sensibly, men just go for a girl who is available; they don't thrive on neglect, like women and pot plants, at all.

For the first time in years I became less focused on men. I realised it was ridiculous to expect someone else to make me happy — this was entirely up to me. I also began to see a clear pattern in my relationships. I would find myself again and again being attracted to unavailable men but when they responded I would lose interest.

Perhaps this blueprint began early. My parents divorced when I was 8 and from that time my relationship with my adored father became more distant and erratic. As I got older I became hurt and resentful at the inconsistency of our relationship. I longed for his attention which blew hot and cold. He remained the gold standard as far as men were concerned (Electra had it easy!) and it was very hard for boyfriends to live up to this idealised version of supposedly masculine perfection I had hardwired into my brain. I realised that it would be difficult to have a good relationship with a boyfriend until I could sort out all of this. Until then I was going round in circles.

Buddhism emphasises the importance of harmonious family relationships. It's crucial to get these right before we can have successful relationships with others, so this is what I determined to do. It was the start of three years without a sniff of a boyfriend, but maybe that was just as well. Maybe it was now time to put the emphasis on something else.

Meanwhile, my second novel, *Chalet Tiara,* had come out and sold modestly so I decided to have another bash at journalism and got busy pitching articles to features editors. Depressingly, idea after idea was rejected. Months went by with no work. It was crushing. But it hadn't always been like this. During my brief flourishing of It-girlitis I'd often been commissioned by the *Daily Mail, Tatler* and countless other publications. Was I burnt up already?

And then I came across an article about life coach Fiona

Harrold, who had apparently performed miraculous feats helping people to revitalise their careers. Thinking she'd be far too busy and well known to take me on, I was surprised, after I'd explained my situation, that she jumped at the challenge.

'What can I do?' I moaned. 'I'm trying so hard. I'm thinking of packing it all in and moving to Hawaii!'

This was true. For many years I'd been looking for a good excuse to emigrate to the Kahala Mandarin Oriental in Oahu, a wonderful hotel where my father and I had once enjoyed a fantastic holiday. It was one of the very rare occasions when we'd spent time together and I had associated Hawaii with all things magical ever since.

The Kahala was pricey but I reckoned if I sold my flat I could live there on the proceeds for about ten years, a bit like Margaret, the Duchess of Argyll, who lived at the Savoy for fifty years until she died in situ, her famous porcelain complexion quite intact; home owners have far more stress and wrinkles. She was of course quite penniless — but you can't take it with you. Unless you're Warren Buffett, of course.

Maybe now was the perfect time to cut my losses? I could feel the sun in my face and the swaying of palm trees in the warm breeze ...

'Don't be ridiculous!' Fiona thundered, 'If you're not getting what you want it's because you're not doing enough!'

This was interesting. Perhaps I hadn't been trying as hard as I thought I had. I am easily disheartened and had magnified each rejection into monstrous proportions. Like Edison, the inventor of the light bulb, I realised I must increase my failure rate. When we hear about successful people we don't hear so much about their fight up the greasy pole — we often assume success just lands in their laps. But the difference between someone whose dreams have come true and someone whose dream hasn't is often sheer determination, sweat and effort.

So I redoubled my efforts. I had more ideas and emailed them into the ether. One day, thinking what the hell, he's probably too busy to see all his emails, I pitched an idea to Simon Kelner, editor of *The Independent*.

Several days later I got a call from his secretary who said Simon wanted to interview me over lunch for his restaurant column in *GQ* magazine. Well you could have blown me down. There was no mention of my green column idea, but I had an in — I could badger him over lunch.

We met at a fancy restaurant at the top of a vast skyscraper in the City, popular with tycoons and bankers. The menu was awful, stuff like crocodile steak, ostrich tartare and pig's trotters — crap that must impress City boys. But I didn't care — I had the undivided attention of an influential newspaper editor and it was heaven. Simon was cheerful and easy to talk to, so after our jolly lunch, emboldened by lack of food and a surfeit of champagne, I seized my chance on the way out.

'How about I do a green column for the *Indy*?' I asked cheekily, expecting a knock back.

'Yes, why not,' he replied, disappearing into his chauffeur driven Jag. 'I'll get someone to call you.'

Amazingly enough, a few days later someone did. After years of trying I had a column at last. Just like that. It was one of the best things that had ever happened to me — I loved researching and writing different green stories every week. Finally I could do something to raise awareness about all the issues that gave me sleepless nights.

Other commissions soon followed. Fiona wasn't waving a magic wand, but she had got me thinking more positively and, crucially, taking more action.

There was plenty to write about. With a general election coming up I joined the Green Party hoping to be of use canvassing or knocking on doors. Tracking down the local party in Kensington and Chelsea I was surprised to discover it consisted of only one member, Hugo Charlton, a friend from my premarital days.

Hugo is now a barrister but in those days was an impecunious deb's delight/mini-cab driver, so short of funds he lived off canapés from the cocktail party circuit. He used to keep an old ice cream container in the recesses of his dinner jacket into which he squashed vast quantities of quails eggs, miniscule Yorkshire puddings, smoked salmon cartwheels and bits of tinned pineapple on sticks which congealed to make a sort of terrine. Slices of this mixture kept him going for weeks.

His diet appeared to have caused no lasting damage and he had settled down to a life of domesticity with his young family. The appetiser and asparagus cartwheel days were now a distant memory.

I soon realised joining such a small party was a speedy way to be fast tracked. Indeed, as soon as I joined I was asked to be the candidate in Kensington and Chelsea in the 1997 general election, not because I had any political ability at all, but because I was the only person who was prepared to lose the £1,000 deposit required to stand. The deposit would only be returned if I got 2.5 per cent of the votes — fat chance in this true blue heartland presided over by the dashing Michael Portillo.

To celebrate my selection I bought a variety of short, green dresses and persuaded politically inclined girlfriends to come leafleting with me. This was a bad idea as they were far more interested in chatting up handsome Italian and French bankers strolling down the King's Road, but these suave fellows were of no use to me at all, as they were not allowed to vote in general elections. Dishearteningly it was left to me to pick up the slack — the elderly, the plain and men with beards.

I hoped to have more success when Hugo and I set up a stall outside Chelsea Town Hall. From there we dispensed green cocktails made from Chartreuse (a foul-tasting bright green liqueur made from herbal extracts by Belgian monks) — raided from his mother's mouldering drinks cabinet — and champagne, garnished with a sprig of organic mint from my roof terrace.

We were soon crushed by a stampede of winos that tottered down from World's End on the rumour of free booze. In the melee a fight broke out causing our trestle table to collapse while the pavement became a sea of green liquid, soggy leaflets and smashed glass. Insisting we were a hazard to the public, a town clerk moved us on.

Maddeningly the other candidates all seemed to be having far more successful campaigns. As well as Mr Portillo, who really didn't have to do anything at all in this truest of blue boroughs, I had competition from the legendary Lord Biro, representing the No Fruit Out of Context Party. Ginger Crab was a charming red-headed fellow who strode about Chelsea wearing a large shell strapped to his back demanding rights for redheads. The Hand Party also created a stir as they drove round town in a car with a huge hand strapped to the top.

By this time I knew I'd never make it as a politician. I'm not a people person, so having to talk to perfect strangers was awful — I find it enough of a struggle to talk to people I know. Besides, you can't walk down the King's Road these days without being set upon by hordes of grinning chuggers (irritating young people employed by charities to sign up unwary pedestrians), and I couldn't bear the thought of adding to the many annoyances of shopping in central London.

I wasn't entirely idle, though, as I ended up employing a team of helpful Poles who, for a small fee, willingly knocked on doors and delivered my election leaflets for me. Whether they were 'on message' concerning the Green cause I'm not quite sure, but it didn't make much difference as none of them spoke English, but I thought I should give them a chance anyway.

Being blonde (I was getting blonder all the time) and under 90, in a world where there are so few women, meant I attracted a lot of attention, most of it the wrong kind. Despite one of the old Green Party mottos being 'not left, not right but forward' — which I thought pretty good and much better than the dreary 'real progress' slogan we've since adopted — there was a lefty feminist faction led by a glamorous white witch in Norfolk who started an enthusiastic campaign to get rid of me.

These lefties were tearing their hair out at the trivial press coverage I was attracting. Mischievous party rightists, a troublesome faction who wanted a leader instead of the dubious and confusing party speaker (a Green Party invention denoting someone who represents the Greens in the media yet is not exactly a leader per se), seized on me with glee, sticking my glossy pic on the cover of the party rag.

Inside I was described in breathy Tatleresque terms as 'the It-girl daughter of X and the granddaughter of X'. It was tongue-in-cheek but the politically correct lefties were livid.

Fortunately many in the party fed up with being laughed at for being bearded, humourless and sandally thought getting some light-hearted press coverage added a bit of balance.

But even I thought things had gone a bit too far when

fearsome hackette Jan Moir — an amusing writer but an awkward person to talk to, as she had an unusual optic disorder (one of her eyes appeared to whiz distractingly around its socket which made it hard to have a rational conversation) — came to interview me for *The Telegraph*. The resulting article was such a fearsome stitch-up my heart sunk with despair.

'I'm the voice of those that cannot speak!' shrieked the headline, referring to my animal welfare campaigns. So embarrassing! Surely even I wouldn't have said something like that in public? Terrible phrases like 'now the only parties I'm interested in are political parties' littered the article. It was illustrated with a picture of me grinning beatifically and shoving my embonpoint (artificially enhanced with a Wonderbra) at a bemused Chelsea pensioner.

I was coming to realise that you can either be a socialite or a worthy; you certainly can't be both. A green, morally responsible It-girl who composts her kitchen waste and doesn't like socialising? How could this be possible? But caricatures belong to fiction and the media. In the real world we are all shades of grey and less easy to define.

Since then I've served my sentence at the political coalface, representing the Greens in two general elections and three council elections but I'm increasingly disillusioned with the political process. With the UK political system so unfairly staked against small parties, and without proportional representation, it's a real struggle for a small party like the Greens — who take no donations from big business (unlike the three main parties) — to have the funds and manpower to make an inroad.

While it is vital for the green-minded to vote for the Green Party — even if you think they haven't a hope, a sizeable minority vote will at least send a signal to the ruling party that there are votes in green policies — these days I prefer being involved with direct action pressure groups like Friends of the Earth and Greenpeace and with supporting local issues. Banding together with friends and neighbours to support a local shop, post office, school or hospital, or to fight against a hypermarket which will put local shops out of business, often has very successful results and unites communities with a common goal. Meanwhile individuals get the chance to discover talents and ingenuity they never thought they had.

Besides, with the main political parties talking about global warming in abstract terms but doing nothing in real terms to make a difference, I felt the best way for me to make an impact was to green up my life, write about it and hopefully inspire others to do the same.

Despite being active within the Green Party and writing a column about green issues I hadn't done a massive amount to actually green up myself. I talked the talk but didn't really walk the walk. By most people's standards I seemed very green, but the green bar was still set quite low — it's only in recent years that awareness has grown hugely.

But I ate mainly organic, my cleaning products were homemade, I consumed very little meat, I recycled everything I could, I reused envelopes, refused all packaging and kept a string bag with me at all times so I didn't have to use plastic ones. So I reclaimed my *Good Life* dream — dormant since my rural experiment and bitter divorce. I was a city girl through and through but I still longed to grow my own vegetables, compost, put up solar panels and wind turbines and be self-sufficient in my energy needs.

I also wanted to convert my loft into an extra room and challenged myself to do this in the most eco-friendly way possible. This would mean tracking down the best organic paints, the most suitable eco-friendly and reclaimed materials — like sheep's wool insulation, cork, vintage fixtures and fittings, plus hemp bricks.

The Good Life in Chelsea! Why not? Plus, I could honestly describe the ups and downs of my plan every week in *The Independent*; by sharing my mistakes and successes I hoped to make it easier for others to have a go too.

But there was no getting away from the fact there were heaps of guilty green secrets, and receipts from Easy Jet, concealed in the depths of my reusable string bag. And there were other green black holes. I kept forgetting to turn off my appliances at the mains. I drove a car. I flew in aeroplanes — taking on average three long-haul flights a year and four short-haul.

I was still suffering from the affluenza virus (although my association with Buddhism was helping my symptoms lessen) but the condition still necessitated many wasted hours on eBay tracking down elusive Birkin handbags (their scarcity and expense makes them tantalisingly desirable) and even longer trawling property websites. I'd moved house five times in ten years, always feeling the next place would be better, even though it usually wasn't, and after I'd completed renovating my current flat I fantasised about moving again to a riverside penthouse, or a beach hut in Whitstable, or maybe even Switzerland.

Moving house is of course stressful but it is also environmentally destructive — every time a house changes hands perfectly good kitchens and bathrooms are ripped out and thrown away, and yet renovation is now a national obsession. It's just another example of the race to accumulate which is destroying our spirit and the planet. Yet it's so easy to be sucked into the chase without thinking about it.

I soon realised there are two green tribes. The vanity 'lite greens', of which I was a member, buy into the whole green lifestyle not necessarily out of a burning concern for the planet's health but mainly because it's better for their health. Fortunately what is good for the planet is usually good for people — but not always …

While the green lites are slaves to their Dr Hauschka rose face cream (made from biodynamically farmed roses which can only be picked when the farm workers are feeling happy) which is great, they undo their greenie points by taking 'eco' holidays in obscure parts of the world that can only be reached by sixteen hours in a gas-guzzling plane.

The green lites (of whom David Cameron is patron saint) spend large sums in the pursuit of eco-chic, buying whatever high anti-oxidant food is top of the health charts that month. Their huge Maytag fridge-freezers groan with blueberries from New Zealand, Goji berries from the Himalayas and Fijian water.

They relax wearing pricey, recycled plimsolls with green laces and employ wildly fashionable 'ecotects' (a term coined by Rachel Johnson in her witty book about life in Notting Hill) to 'green up' their homes (*mea culpa* — not only do I have a Maytag but I'm employing David Cameron's ecotect, but bear with me), contributing to a feeling that eco-living is expensive, about acquiring more stuff and beyond the reach of ordinary mortals.

'Dark greens' are motivated by a far more laudable concern for the planet and I wanted to be like them. Unlike vanity greens their eco-consciousness saves them money, as they are forever switching off lights, growing their own food, not buying things they don't need and avoiding flying. If the best things in life are free they are often green too. Frugal wartime living has been out of fashion since, well, the war, but fortunately the whole string-saving way of life is now very much in vogue.

Anyway my plan was to switch from green lite to deep olive. But I needed advice. It was time to track down a team of eco-experts to green up me and my flat from top to bottom. But this was easier said than done. It's difficult for an ordinary person to know where to start. Fortunately I came across the excellent *How to Save the Planet without Costing the Earth* by eco-auditor Donnachadh McCarthy. I was so impressed by his easy-to-read guide, jammed with loads of money-saving green tips, I booked him for a visit. Here was a true eco-savant and I was eager to scour his brains for advice.

In my blissful ignorance I felt a smug glow of advance approval at how impressed he would be with all the organic food in my cupboards and my Dr Hauschka potions. And no doubt he would swoon at the sight of all my biodynamic champagne stockpiled on the balcony.

How wrong I was.

Chapter 5

The dating jungle

DONNACHADH arrived one freezing morning on a bike. He was a wiry, energetic Irishman with a strong accent which became increasingly impenetrable when he pointed out some outrageous form of eco-wastage in my flat. Here was the real deal — someone who really walked the talk and was devoting his life to improving his patch of the world.

Many people probably feel a bit defensive at the thought of being eco-coached. No one likes the thought of a worthy stranger rifling about in their fridge, bathroom and kitchen cabinets for eco-nasties. It's like some terrible exam which you know you can't possibly pass.

Fortunately Donnachadh is not remotely pious or holier than thou and has a sense of mischief and humour — qualities you definitely need if you're going to be poking around in a stranger's kitchen cupboards.

During my eco-audit Donnachadh boosted me by focusing on the positive. All the organic food went down well (though the Himalayan Goji berries received short shrift). He reminded me that it's better to buy non-organic local rather than long-distance organic — for starters, how do we know what sort of organic standards there are in Peru, for example? Local food is fresher, probably tastes better, supports beleaguered British farmers and has a lower carbon footprint. It just makes sense to eat British food in season.

He awarded me top marks for my waste strategy; indeed when it comes to rubbish I am top of the form. I recycle what I can while all vegetable matter and cardboard is deposited in my worm compost bin, which within months is transformed magically into gorgeous crumbly compost that houseplants adore.

The only trouble is that it takes up too much space on my terrace so I've sneakily dumped it onto my adjoining neighbour's flat roof. He is an elegant, balding banker and I have dreadful visions of my weighty bins collapsing through his roof and landing on his head. I hope I can convince him that a worm toupee is a small price to pay for doing his bit to reduce the nation's waste.

I find the idea of worms transforming kitchen leftovers irresistible and I'm getting delusions of grandeur à la Napoleon. What's to stop me colonising all the unused flat roofs in my terrace and setting up miles of worm factories on them? At this rate I'll turn into the Bernard Matthews of worm farming.

Donnachadh was less keen on my huge Maytag fridge and freezer. It's probably a bit excessive for a single person who hates entertaining. To be fair, the fridge is always quite full — unlike the half-empty deep freeze which he suggested filling with empty cartons and packaging because a full fridge and deep freeze uses less energy, and reduces electricity bills.

Things nosedived further when he came face to face with my Bang and Olufson stereo system that can't be turned off at the mains without the entire system having to be reset and thus must remain on standby at all times. I don't know what made me invest in the whole macho B and O thing. I am not a merchant banker and do not want to impress women. And now I find myself lumbered with this system which probably keeps Sellafield in business. Eight to ten per cent of the total electricity currently used in the home is due to appliances left on standby. If we switched off properly and stopped wasting energy at work, as well as at home, the threat of building more nuclear power stations might be avoided.

My light bulbs got short shrift too but they were more easily dealt with. Donnachadh suggested replacing them with low energy bulbs which use eighty per cent less electricity. They last around twelve times longer than conventional bulbs which will save a whopping £65 over the lifespan of each bulb.

In an immediate bid to reduce my wasteful lighting he removed several spotlights from the bathroom and bedroom. While these rooms still had enough light to see in, the gaping holes left were not attractive and as soon as he left I confess I whipped the bulbs back in.

At least I'm signed up to Good Energy, an energy provider which sources its electricity from renewable sources. I now see that it doesn't cost very much to make profound changes. It's not all about wind turbines and expensive solar systems. Simple actions like turning off lights, putting on an extra jersey rather than switching on the gas fire, and switching off the oven ten minutes before food is cooked (modern ovens are so well insulated they will continue cooking) would have an enormous impact if we all made the effort.

For further inspiration Donnachadh invited me to his eco-cottage in Camberwell to show me what can be done. It appears he's even more of a rubbish queen than me — by avoiding packaging and recycling he has no dustbin, and swears that he throws away only one bag of rubbish a year. The only thing I forgot to ask is how big is this bag? It might be huge. Anyway, I shall soon find out …

A few weeks later I pitched up at Donnachadh's Victorian cottage to find green nirvana and self-sufficiency of the highest order. A solar hot water system supplies about seventy per cent of the household's hot water needs, while solar electric panels produce so much power that he actually exports electricity back to the national grid.

A large tank on his roof collects rainwater which is used for flushing the loo and watering the garden. He creates minimal waste — he's not lying when he told me he creates one bag of rubbish a year and, yes, it's a very small bag. His food is delivered every week from a local health food cooperative with returnable packaging. The dreaded hard-to-recycle tetra cartons are avoided as he makes his own soya and rice milk with a soya milk maker, his kitchen leftovers go on the compost heap and he just doesn't buy excess stuff.

Unfortunately I couldn't stay for very long as he had to race out for a naked gay yoga session. I'm not giving away any state secrets here — in fact he's happy for me to mention his social proclivities as he believes it is important people see that greens are multi-faceted and not totally mired in doom and gloom. And being gay is greener than being heterosexual, as you're not likely to give birth. With the world's population now at six billion, and many of them wanting to experience the carbon-busting delights of electricity and cheap flights, a sure fire way for us all to halt the planet's demand for energy is to go gay and not produce any more children.

It's interesting that when we discuss reducing carbon emissions much of the focus is quite rightly on cutting down on our flights. However there are other forms of carbon consumption — population control and energy use at home, for example — that create more carbon emissions and are escalating. Unfortunately no Western government would dare suggest we keep the birth rate down to one or two children per couple, even though reducing the population of the developed world would mean a huge reduction in emissions.

Commentators usually suggest that the focus should be on reducing birth rates in Africa and India, but the average carbon footprint of someone in the developing world is far less than his or her equivalent in the West, so more emphasis should be on making us aware of the need to reduce population growth. The ironic thing is that many environmentalists have a higher birth rate than the rest of the population. I don't mention this to criticise — munificently my lack of ability to breed coincides with zero maternal instincts, so any greenie points are by sheer accident.

The fertility of environmentalists is fascinating though. Does altruism by some sort of Darwinian principle increase fertility or does their healthy organic diet make them more fertile? (It doesn't work for me.) Notable environmentalists with growing hordes of progeny include Zac Goldsmith who has three, Bobby Kennedy Jr in the best Catholic tradition has six and Leo Hickman three. Donnachadh and green writer Will Anderson, who built his own eco-house from scratch, have none, but then they are gay. Hopefully they will resist the current baby mania and not go for the surrogate mother option — no use looking at me, chaps.

French writer Corinne Maier holds similarly forthright views. She wrote the controversial polemic *No Kid: 40 Reasons Not to Have Children* (what, only forty?), in which she bravely defies the current bout of baby mania by suggesting that having children is environmentally destructive as well as 'boring'. She reckons she'd have had a far more interesting life if she'd never had any herself. Then instead of stacking washing machines and getting up at the crack of dawn to do the school run she could be writing more books and having a far jollier time all round. Of course, if she'd been British she could have bunged them into boarding school, then she could have had her cake and ate it, but there you go.

So while hordes of childless women are going through the tortuous process of IVF, freezing their eggs and having random unprotected sex with drunken strangers, she is encouraging them to think again. Maier believes that the wealthy West is producing too many children, which is speeding up the depletion of the world's resources. 'It's not that there are too many people,' she writes, 'but too many rich people. No one needs our children, because we and they are the spoilt kids of a planet that is on a collision course. To have a child in Europe or America is immoral — scarcer resources wasted on a way of life that is ever more voracious, capricious, hungry for fuel and destructive of the environment.'

However, for many people, having a child is as instinctive as the desire for food and shelter but there is no getting around the fact that bringing a new person into the packed planet is the least eco-friendly thing you can do.

Thank goodness then that there are people who selflessly choose to adopt one of the thousands of unwanted children already in the world. I admire Madonna and Angelina Jolie for their commitment to adoption but it's unfair that the former gets so much flack when both Angelina Jolie and Mia Farrow attracted barely any criticism for their adoption marathons — Mia Farrow has to date adopted an astonishing eleven children, and good for her.

I didn't know much about Mia Farrow except that she went to Rishikesh with the Beatles where the Maharishi made advances to her in a cave (I'm not sure if she ever recovered) but since reading her autobiography I am full of admiration for her astonishing feats of childcare.

Personally, I can barely cope with the strain of being a godmother even though I barely see my godchildren from one year to the next. I don't know why I keep saying yes — a mixture of vanity and hope that this time I'll do a better job.

Many childless women complain that their barren state is made even harder by general disapproval and accusations of being selfish, but I've had no experience of this — I think people would be far more disapproving if I did get pregnant. Only once did someone try to convince me of the error of my ways by saying 'but your child might find the solution to global warming!'

I fear any child of mine would probably suffer from terrible emotional ishoos and would be unlikely to find the solution to anything, but of course, I shall never know, which may be just as well. Besides, knowing my luck I'd end up with a real petrol-head — children always rebel against their parents.

Meanwhile, I am gripped by the many weepy articles, often in the *Daily Mail,* written by 30-something women agonising about not meeting Mr Right in time to breed, or infertile couples undergoing intrusive courses of IVF. I read these with a large dollop of *schadenfreude* and feel hugely grateful that while I've often felt dissatisfied in most other spheres of my life, this at least was one area in which I was happy with my lot. We may wonder if we'll miss out on some wonderful experience if we don't have a family, but having children or not having children is no guarantee of happiness in itself. It's up to the individual to make the most of the hand they are dealt.

Finally, lazy girls have the perfect excuse when asked why they don't have children by broody potential grandmothers. We are childfree, of course, for the sake of the planet.

Not because we are too idle, hate getting up early and would much prefer a brood of Shetland sheepdogs.

So, without distractions on the domestic front I was free to take up a run of wonderful commissions from the *Daily Mail.* Up to this point I'd been busy with my column, but this was now taking less time to write so it was great to be offered other work. The *Mail* sent me to Faliraki — then considered to be the Sodom and Gomorrah of the Med — to report on the sexual and alcoholic excesses of Britain's corrupted yoof. Unfortunately the dreaded yoofs had behaved impeccably, so there was no story. Nick, the photographer, and I had dutifully gone out every night desperate for pictures of vomiting in the streets and mass fornication but to our disappointment all we ever found were well-behaved librarians and public schoolgirls. It seemed we were a few years too late — all the real action had moved on to Ibiza.

Then they'd asked me to write something about top-end dating agencies and reply to some small ads in upmarket publications. I threw myself into the project with an open mind, deciding to advertise myself in the *Sunday Times* dating column:

> *Blonde authoress and eco warrior, religious but not spiritual,*
> *seeks older, richer, taller man for inspiration for current novel.*
> *Please send photograph of house.*

Obviously I wanted to see the house; I didn't want some chap who lived in a tepee for God's sake. Plus, I'd added the 'religious but not spiritual' bit as a foil to the irritating 'spiritual but not religious' box that seems to appear increasingly in the faith section of forms these days, for those too feeble to commit themselves to a proper religion. So flaky!

Even an atheist is preferable to this lot, who think having a massage while listening to whale music or reading Paulo Coelho's soppy mystical allegory *The Alchemist* will lead them to enlightenment.

I was soon deluged with endless photos of yachts, Tuscan farmhouses and mansions, unfortunately attached to rather uninspiring owners. But one game fellow had been snapped outside Blenheim Palace. Full marks for trying but I must confess I wasn't tempted to follow up on any of them.

Another 'exclusive' website set me up with a bankrupt kitchen fitter with a harelip (poor fellow) and on the best website of the lot for this sort of thing (and the cheapest, Match.com) I'd met a staggeringly handsome pilot who I couldn't believe would need to join an agency — surely all he had to do was stomp up and down the airplane with his pilot's hat on and women would have swooned in the aisles. But it soon became obvious that he was staggeringly dull, hence the need to advertise. Just as well I wasn't (very) tempted — an eco-worrier and a pilot was hardly a match made in heaven.

But if these were the sort of men who reckoned they were top of the pile, who knew what might lurk at the bottom? Meeting a wonderful man from the dating personals is like seeing a ghost — everyone knows someone who has, but nobody has actually seen one for themselves.

It was a relief to file my article and give up the man hunt. It was tiring, stressful and took up so much time. How on earth did anyone fit in dating with a full-time job? Although I was happy being single I did vaguely think it would be nice to meet someone, but hopefully he would just fall into my lap, so to speak, without me actually having to comb the streets looking for him.

I celebrated my release from dating duty by persuading

an air stewardess pal, Connie, to fly (no letters, please) with me to Toronto and attend a lecture given by the world's most handsome environmentalist, Bobby Kennedy. In retrospect, the carbon emissions were inexcusable, but this was in 2005, six months before it became politically incorrect to fly. I paid US$30 to go to a sparsely attended private reception beforehand, along with a bunch of Canadian transvestites, various Kennedy fanatics and one enormous nun. When it came to my turn to shake his hand I was so overcome by his charisma and extreme sex appeal that my knees buckled and I was quite unable to speak. My carefully rehearsed chat about the plight of North American pigs (or hogs as they are rather grimly known in the US) was quite wasted. It wouldn't have done any good anyway as he was soon transfixed by a sexy girl with the deepest, gravelliest voice I've ever heard. She had legs like milk bottles but it was scant consolation nonetheless.

Although he is very married with hordes of children, I was cast down that he hadn't even flirted with me. Had I been celibate for so long that my sex hormones had withered away completely? Secretly I fretted that I'd lost the healthy, happy, pheremony glow you need to attract someone in the first place. I do think it imperative to be out there practising your game, so to speak, so that when the right chap comes along you are in peak flirting condition. But I obviously hadn't been practising enough.

In darker moments I wondered, like Bridget Jones, if I was doomed to a lonely old age before being savaged by an Alsatian and discovered months later by the postman (unless he'd been on strike, in which case I might never get found at all).

Chapter 6

No good deed goes unpunished

FORTUNATELY, as soon as I got home from Canada I was distracted from the miserable prospect of my dwindling pheromones by an offer to write a fierce article about the appalling conditions of factory farmed pigs.

I'd been an animal rights campaigner since childhood and for many years I'd been a vegetarian. Avoiding or at least cutting back on meat is one of the most environmentally friendly things we can do. As well as the appalling cruelty involved in intensive meat production, silage spill-off pollutes land and rivers, while somewhat unexpectedly, methane from cattle is the largest cause of global warming. Meanwhile, the desperately needed green lung of the Amazon is constantly being razed to create land and food for livestock. So when Viva!, an animal rights charity which I supported, invited me to break into a Berkshire factory farm at midnight to film undercover footage with them I knew I'd get a good story.

The irony of being a vegetarian animal rightist and a member of the Vestey family — whose fortune is generated from the meat industry — gave the story a stronger hook. I've never had any qualms about using family connections to raise publicity for animal abuses — much to the chagrin of my family it must be said.

Breaking in was a horrifying experience. I took Hugo along too — as a barrister I felt he might save our bacon should we be surprised by an irate farmer with a sawn-off shotgun.

Once inside we discovered fetid, stinking sheds full of sows crammed into small crates for weeks at a time. Dead piglets littered the ground, rats ran over my feet and the stench and heat were unbearable. It was a writhing mass of suffering — like a Hieronymus Bosch painting come to life.

The *Mail* splashed the story over two pages with the dramatic header: 'The terrible truth behind the business that made my family its fortune.'

It didn't stop there. Radio 4 invited me on to *Start the Week* to discuss it and I mentioned that Smithfield, the world's largest pork producer, has built huge American-style 'hog factories' in Poland. From there they are flooding European supermarkets — including one in the UK, which I had the temerity to mention — with cheap meat.

After the show someone from Radio 4 rang me in quite a state saying that this supermarket's switchboard was being flooded by outraged customers preparing to boycott the store, which was now threatening to sue me. It gave me a nasty turn but fortunately it all blew over and that was the last I heard of it. But it is common knowledge that Smithfield Foods in Poland still supplies British supermarkets with cheap pork, pumping the countryside with raw sewage and squeezing local farmers with higher welfare standards out of business.

It is a tragedy for animals and people that this company is now being given grants to expand by the EU. Poland is historically made up of small family farms which are home to rare wildlife such as white storks and bison. Its unpolluted soil and sparkling rivers were once known as the purest in Europe.

British pig farmers have some of the highest welfare standards in Europe (OK, this isn't saying that much) but welfare doesn't come cheap. Tragically, the British consumer's insatiable demand for cheap pork means they end up buying cut-price poor quality pork from countries with appalling welfare standards, thereby putting British pig farmers out of business. It's easy to blame governments and corporations but ultimately it's up to us, the consumer, to fight for change; he who pays the piper calls the tune.

I hoped to make these points when I was invited on to a television news programme presented by an ex-crush of mine, the charming but libidinous Al Robson. Terrifyingly, I was to debate factory farming with a Suffolk pig farmer. But I was far more alarmed by the prospect of meeting up with Al for whom I had nursed a crush since he'd invited me to a boozy but very high profile BBC party. I'd gone along with a girlfriend and on arrival we were introduced to a self-important government minister but found ourselves so distracted by a slew of dandruff on his expensively tailored suit we couldn't concentrate on what he was saying. How wonderful to have such intractable self-belief that such hideous realities pass one by. We escaped as soon as we could and joined a group held agog by a shifty and dishevelled foreign correspondent boasting about his fearless travels. His audience was spellbound but my eyes glazed over as he described foiling a recent kidnap attempt in some detail.

'In Iraq?' breathed my friend reverently.

'No, outside John Lewis.' He glanced nervously over his shoulder and his face froze in terror. 'I've got to get out of here! My boss', he nodded at Al, 'is giving me filthy looks. He didn't like a report I filed last week …' I looked over at Al who was tipping back whisky and bumming a cigarette off Ken Clarke, then Minister for Health. The words 'my boss' and the fear in his eyes made a light bulb go off in my head. I'd always thought of Al as nothing more than an amusing and scruffy joker, despite being the producer of a respected news show, but now I could see I'd underestimated him. Anyone who was capable of inspiring such fear had to be a force to be reckoned with.

As I had a thing for powerful but unattainable men who reminded me of my distant but charming father, this activated my Electra complex immediately. Before we left I gave him my email address and soon after he invited me out and we'd had a drunken snog in a wine bar. Then he'd invited me to an awful lunch at the *Spectator*, where I'd sat next to the editor of *The Times*.

'What do you do?' I asked this august fellow.

'I'm the editor of *The Times*,' he replied patiently.

I thought light relief might be provided by the *Spectator*'s then editor, Boris Johnson, but no such luck. When we were introduced I suggested, tongue-in-cheek, that the Conservatives should pick up and run with green issues (you must understand that this was in the Michael Howard days, way before the touchy-feely hug-a-hoodie Cameron era).

'Ah yes!' he boomed. 'We must put the Conserve back into the Conservative party!' This was the cue for my (fortunately) fake pearl necklace to break and the cheapo — but very realistic — 'pearls' scattered across the creaky wooden floor. Instead of coming to my aid, Boris looked terrified (maybe he could tell they were fake) then scuttled off into the famous *Spectator* dining room — a rather small, moth-eaten wooden room that reminded me of school.

During lunch — a great bloody slab of beef, so macho! — a small sweating guest (actually it was me) asked conversationally if he was half German. He snapped, 'You're thinking of Boris Becker,' while some of his toadies sniggered meanly at my gaffe. Now, Boris Becker is a six foot two inch ripplingly muscled Teutonic SEX GOD. There was no way even I, with my terrible eyesight, could confuse him with the short, portly magazine editor across the table shovelling steak into his mouth. It was the worst lunch of my life and I left as soon as I could.

The TV show was predictably terrifying, even though the pig farmer had been pleasant and non-confrontational. But I got tongue-tied, so thank heavens Al stepped in and boosted my cause. Then he spent the rest of the show handing out bacon sarnies. Bizarrely, his scary sidekick, Kate Silverton, turned to me at the end, apropos of nothing, and said, 'Well, we can't all drive Lamborghinis you know.'

Despite my feeble appearance Viva! was grateful and made me a patron (no good deed goes unpunished) and sent out a press release which began: 'Julia is better known as a shallow shopping socialite …' I wish, I thought, reading it flat out after a long day protesting at Huntington Life Sciences Laboratory. I may be shallow but I'm hardly a socialite. 'But she has now turned her back on the high life …' It wasn't that I'd turned my back on the high life. Rather it had turned its back on me. Still. Whatever.

Becoming a charity patron is a bit like being a godmother. It is flattering to be seen as compassionate and capable enough to take on the responsibility, but I never felt I was doing enough to merit the honour. Indeed, I was far more active before I was made a patron — guilt immobilised me. Similarly when Emma, a close pal, got pregnant I was a staunch support. I visited her in hospital, brought her everything she needed and after the birth dispensed presents and encouragement. I knew if it was me undergoing birth with no support from the father I'd desperately need my friends to support me.

The trouble was that as a reward she offered me the post of godmothership. Oddly enough, having a few good turns legalised in this way made me want to run for the hills. I could now understand men pushing off at the first sign of a positive pregnancy test. From then on I felt expectation weigh heavily on my shoulders; this was a lifetime commitment, something I'd always been keen to avoid.

It was the same with being made a patron of Viva! And ironically, soon after being ennobled, I'd started to eat animal products occasionally. The two activities weren't linked but after many years of blameless vegetarianism I'd suddenly begun to crave meat and cheese. It was guilt-making but I could literally feel that first mouthful of fillet steak, bought at the farmers' market from a biodynamic butcher, soak into my gasping cells. Although I feel healthier for eating meat very occasionally I have no desire to become a poster girl for carnivorism. For those who suit a vegan diet, and I know many who thrive on it, that's fantastic. But it is imperative that the rest of us find out exactly the provenance of our meat and eat it in reduced quantities, paying a lot more than we currently do to guarantee the highest welfare.

There isn't a satisfactory word to describe those of us who eat ethically farmed meat very rarely, but the admirable campaigning group Compassion in World Farming set up an Eat Less Meat Campaign in 2004, as they believe encouraging die-hard carnivores to cut down is more effective then telling them to give up meat completely. Though with developing nations stratospherically increasing their demand for cheap meat, more of us becoming vegans can only be a good thing in balancing out demand.

These days I eat meat about once a week from a local farm and savour every mouthful. I avoid meat in restaurants, hotels, when travelling and still won't touch pork, as the thought of it makes my stomach turn. But having been so famously a vegetarian I was in a dilemma. Most cowardly I kept putting off telling Viva! While I respected the good job they did in promoting welfare issues in the media, I was getting fed up with the way they kept banging on about my tenuous Vestey connections. On one hand you can see the necessity of doing anything to expose the cruelty of battery farming but the grumbles of ancient uncles in the shires har-rumphing about bringing the family unwanted publicity was embarrassing all the same. Eventually I bit the bullet and told them — it was easier than I thought — and to my relief I was quietly removed from my position as patron, to be replaced by Heather Mills who is able to generate far more publicity than I ever could.

Chapter 7

Lemons are pretty good

I WAS now well into the rhythm of writing my column for *The Independent*. Each piece was a joy to write and nothing brought me more satisfaction than being able to raise awareness of issues close to my heart. It became such a part of my life I couldn't ever imagine not doing it.

Curiously enough, of all the things I discussed, eco-friendly cleaning products generated the biggest postbag. There is an increasing awareness that conventional cleaning fluids expose us to a hazardous cocktail of toxicity. Hundreds of dangerous chemicals, including formaldehyde, phenol and ammonia are regularly used. This is no secret — manufacturers emblazon their products with skulls and crossbones and 'danger' and 'do not inhale' warnings, while painting a picture of a fearsome battle with germs which must be won.

We're not winning this war though, and the overuse of these chemicals has created a raft of immune superbugs like MRSA, which are multiplying and exposing us to real danger. Besides, all these cleaning products usually smell awful, are tested on animals (unless you buy them from sources like Marks & Spencer who have a non-animal testing policy on all their toiletries and cleaning products) and are packaged

ur own which will save money

ny own cleaning products I
es (no men oddly enough)
not making a soufflé for
of neat lemon juice, vin-
ill clean most things.

and bicarbonate of soda sprinkled
baking tray, hot from the oven, will create exciting chemistry lab style froth. Leave this mixture for a few
minutes and the grime will just lift itself off and be washed
away quite easily. Meanwhile, salt and lemon juice will clean
brass very effectively. And if I'm travelling and fear the hotel
will be grubby, I decant my bug-zapping MRSA-proof spray
made from tea tree oil and vodka (patent pending) into an
old spray bottle — it's just the sort of thing Howard Hughes
would have given his right arm for. This is perfect for sterilising dirty hotel bathrooms and it smells delicious too.

The only problem you may have with making your own
cleaning stuff is trying to persuade your cleaner, if you have
one, of the benefits. When I moved into my current flat, I
inherited my saintly cleaning lady, Mrs Pipolotta, who was
simply unable to function without vast quantities of noxious
sprays and used to nick terrifying looking containers bearing
skulls and crossbones from the hospital where she worked.
Despite my pleas over many months, identical cleaning fluids
in different bottles for every conceivable room — even rooms
I didn't have — continued to proliferate in my cupboard. My
loo had never been so blue. (I've noticed that blues, pinks
and greens are popular colours for cleaning materials but
they will never use brown, grey, black or red, presumably
because they are too reminiscent of bodily functions.)

Mrs P was an unreconstructed Ecover-free zone, the last

bastion of guilt-free bleach and aggressive in her use of dangerous cleaning fluids. Soon you will only be able to buy these products in third world dictatorships, where they will flourish along with DDT, heroin and other banned substances.

It took a while but slowly but surely my perseverance paid off and she eventually became similarly evangelical in her use of eco-friendly cleaning products. There was a price, however, to be paid for changing Mrs P's global consciousness, and our chats soon extended into long conversations during which she would bang on about her feckless husband, his bad leg and their barrels of ungrateful children. I soon realised I was suffering from a classic textbook case of CLFS (Cleaning Lady Fatigue Syndrome), first noted by sociologists in the caring nineties when guilty middle class employers, in a pathetic bid to suck up to their cleaners (who were like gold dust — unlike today when we are deluged), transformed into an uneasy mixture of benefactress, confidante and therapist. You may wonder why I didn't find another cleaner. But Mrs P couldn't help being garrulous. Besides, she needed the job, she was thorough and I couldn't face having to indoctrinate another cleaner into my obscure green ways. Meanwhile, I began to escape with my laptop to the library, the gym, the hairdresser — I would tap away during pedicures and train journeys, sometimes I would drive the car to Sainsbury's car park (it had a soothing view of the Thames) and work from there. Thanks to Mrs P I was soon able to work from anywhere.

So, although it was great to be greening up my life on a small scale like this (if everyone in the UK eschewed toxic cleaning products and used natural alternatives it would detoxify our environment on a massive scale — our streams and rivers would be cleaner, there would be less waste and packaging and we would cut down on absorbing noxious chemicals through our skin), I was impatient to get on with my plan to power my home with renewable energy from the sun and wind.

Luckily I now had Donnachadh on hand to give me proper advice. As he had been generating most of his energy from renewable sources for several years, and had a wind turbine on order, he was in a prime position to advise me on the labyrinthine process of getting things underway.

As I wanted to raise the roof slightly and convert my loft into an extra room, I would also need a green-minded architect who could advise on this as well as my proposed renewable energy systems. My prayer was answered when I was flicking through the *Evening Standard* and came across an article about Alex Michaelis and the amazing underground house he has designed for himself in salubrious Notting Hill. It was bright, white and very airy — just what I was looking to achieve for myself — so I gave him a call.

These days Alex has shot into the eco-stratosphere as the celebrated ecotect behind David Cameron's eco-makeover and is on the speed dial of Notting Hill's greenest celebs. The other startling thing about Alex is that he is dazzlingly handsome with matinee idol good looks. This means he is often featured on the cover of groovy design and architectural magazines — I reckon he's got nearly as many covers as Cindy Crawford.

There was no picture of him in the article so I nearly keeled over when this god-like creature strolled into my flat. I made us a cup of sweet tea and calmed down enough to take him up to the roof to discuss where we might put the experimental wind turbines. (I say experimental because domestic wind turbines in cities are currently not effective but leaps in technology may mean that in a few years they do become viable, so it would be good to have planning permission in place just in case.)

Anyway, I was in such a state of excitement (it's not often one gets a gentleman caller of this quality), I thought I might just float off the roof like the wife in many of Chagall's delightful paintings who is always about to drift up into the sky like a balloon. I felt I should tie my foot to a satellite dish to prevent me ascending into the heavens too.

But when we sat down in the sitting room I soon fell to earth. It was a very hot day and I was wearing a sun dress and no tights. As I sat down on the sofa, the friction in my legs somehow conspired cruelly to make a very loud farting sound. I swear it wasn't a real fart; since I've started food combining (I haven't mixed my carbs and proteins for over five years now) I've barely 'let off' at all. But I couldn't say to him, 'Actually that wasn't a fart. Due to the hot weather and skin friction I made a noise that sounded like one, which wasn't in fact any such thing.' Perhaps I could have just said, 'Ooh, a bit windy today.' As if! Anyway, I just thought I would share this incredibly embarrassing vignette with you, to get it off my chest so to speak.

But while we're on the subject of extreme handsomeness, I must point out that greens have now morphed from farty (I swear mine was a one-off), bean-munching, sandal-clad creatures into divine and handsome beings. Alex's business partner, Tim, is also stupendously good-looking, plus there is Zac Goldsmith, Green Party siren Sian Berry, eco-author Will 'handsome' Anderson, who built his own green house from scratch, and of course, my eco-squeeze, S. I wasn't going out with him at this stage so I can't officially mention him just yet. Moving swiftly on, Donnachadh and I brush up pretty well too beneath dim energy-saving bulbs and after the judicious application of Dr Hauschka's biodynamic unguents.

I'm thinking of setting up a model agency to accommodate us all. I could call it Eco Storm.

Now I had Donnachadh and Alex on board it was time to start the long haul of getting planning permission. It seemed ridiculous that here we were trying to do something to conserve energy and reduce carbon emissions, yet we were the ones having to beg permission to do so. No such strenuous tests and permissions needed for those who want to bung tons of carbon into the atmosphere by jumping on planes, use gas-guzzling patio heaters or buy over-packaged green beans from Kenya.

How I wish there were more financial incentives for going green rather than having to rely on our consciences the whole time. Realistically, self-interest is what drives most of us, which must mean green taxes would be an effective way to cut emissions. Taxes on how much rubbish we put out, for example, are a real inducement to recycle and might make us all think a bit more before buying heavily packaged goods.

To get the ball rolling Alex, Donnachadh and I decided to organise a meeting at my flat with two stalwart ladies from the Kensington and Chelsea planning department. Several hours of detailed discussion followed during which their only concern seemed to be that changing my roofline might disturb the skyline (in reality only visible to birds and passengers in very low-flying aircraft).

I could see the chaps were getting restive but not daring to antagonise them we bit our collective lips. We longed to point out that unless we all reduce our energy needs within fifty years my whole street will be underwater and we'll be too busy swimming to give a fig about the skyline.

I didn't point out either that unsightly satellite dishes and mobile phone masts are frequently erected round the country yet need no permission. Phone masts are unpopular and have been implicated in a host of health problems, so it's unfair that they sneak in without planning permission while solar energy systems are subjected to draconian scrutiny. Anyway, I passed around the organic flapjacks, smiled pleasantly and crossed my fingers. The ladies were non-committal when they left but we'd given them our best shot. All we could do now was sit back and wait for the powers that be to make their decision.

Chapter 8

I'm trying to give up flying, really I am ...

HOWEVER, it's one thing reducing your carbon emissions at home by generating your own electricity with solar panels, being super-insulated and reducing your energy needs, but all this can be undone in a stroke if, like me, you maintain a monstrous travel habit.

Flying is a conundrum for many of us greens. Like normal people we long to see the world, indulge ourselves in hot balmy places and in my case, gorge on spiritual shopping experiences and hear handsome environmentalists speak halfway across the world. Yet flying, while not the largest contributor to global warming (as I've mentioned already, population growth and cows are greater contributors), creates four per cent of emissions but is rising fast as the developing world takes to the skies.

Airline emissions are particularly dangerous as they are released very close to the ozone layer. Knowing that every time I fly I'm contributing to rising seas and temperatures which are creating untold devastation to much of the world's population, how on earth can I justify taking a holiday flight, especially as so many lovely places are accessible by train and ferry?

It's extraordinary how awareness has grown in the past two years. A few years ago if you'd suggested that flying would one day be as politically incorrect as eating foie gras, veal or sleeping around without a condom, no one would have taken you seriously, but flying is now seen as a selfish indulgence, with many of us cutting down or at least thinking about it.

The 1980s and 1990s were a time of binge travelling when exotic travel became affordable for the man in the street for the first time. It's similar to the era when the pill had just come on to the market and before the advent of Aids. For the libidinously inclined this brief window of opportunity was the perfect chance to make hay without the grim consequences of fatal disease or pregnancy. But then the emergence of HIV put the fear of God into everyone and the good times were severely curtailed. It's the same for green-minded erstwhile casual flyers; guilt and fear — not of our own imminent demise but that of the planet's — has taken away much of the pleasure.

But not quite all. Back in June 2005 I wrote in my column (foolishly) about a trip to Hawaii and incurred severe displeasure in the letters page the next day. How I paid for my pleasure! Let me explain. In the month before it became environmentally incorrect to fly, I flew there (with just a very small tinge of guilt because these were golden guilt-free days when barely anyone mentioned the dreaded phrase 'carbon emissions'). I planned to write a piece about eco-issues in Hawaii and I also felt duty-bound to mention the swanky hotel I was staying in, as they were giving me a free massage — not just *any* massage you understand but a 'spa ritual' worth hundreds of dollars.

I've since learnt to avoid any treatment that describes itself as a 'spa ritual' or 'spa journey' as it just means they play whale music extra loudly and make you put your feet in a bowl of tepid water with a rose petal floating in it. So even though the spa ritual was very disappointing, I nonetheless felt compelled to give them some puff. So I filed a column about the vast 'plastic soup' of waste in the Pacific Ocean, much of which is washed up on Hawaii's beaches, managing to squeeze in a mention of this wretched spa ritual *en passant*.

But the time the column came out a month later it had become environmentally incorrect to fly and the letters pages were chock-a-bloc with violent diatribes from angry old men. (We are told that women are becoming increasingly angry but old men are permanently furious judging by the letters they write to newspaper columnists — trust me, we swap notes.)

'How can you call yourself the Green Goddess?' livid correspondents thundered. I must admit they were quite right. What was I thinking? I should have just not written about it. Hah!

In confessional mood I must admit in the bad old good old days I used to fly to Hawaii twice a year, to say nothing of many other trips. I whizzed about the world on bargain round-the-world tickets without a thought. It was a bit compulsive. I loved planes. I loved looking at them, the sound of them, sitting in them, eating, drinking and flirting in them. If I'd been born thirty years ago I would have applied to be a Pan Am girl. I guess I was a borderline dromomaniac. Dromomania is an obscure disorder describing people who are so obsessed by travel it becomes a personality disorder. One of my medical dictionaries describes it as 'an uncontrollable impulse to wander or travel'. The Greek origin is *dromos*: running + mania, insanity. It doesn't sound too uncommon a condition to me, or even that bothersome, although flying these days is so ghastly that being a dromomaniac is an increasingly stressful condition.

Fortunately, for green-minded sufferers there is light at the end of the tunnel in the form of the wonderful website, seat61.com, run by ex-British Rail employee Mark Smith, who appears to be surgically attached to every bus, railway and ferry timetable in the world. On it he describes how to reach practically everywhere on the planet without getting on a plane. It's extraordinarily detailed, with photos of cabins, up-to-date timetables, tips and advice.

I also live reasonably close to St Pancras, gateway to Europe since the arrival of the sassy Eurostar terminal with its speedy trains. This fabulous, luxurious, ultra-efficient service opens up the whole continent and beyond. Once you've tried it, air travel seems even more horrible. So I still travel but not so far afield.

I travel regularly to Geneva — now only five hours by train — while it's possible to reach Germany, Belgium and Austria in a day. Although it takes longer than flying, the journey is far more restful than the modern day Hades that is the airport. Like the tortoise and the hare, sometimes the train traveller arrives before the plane passenger once you factor in the regular delays and security alerts. Proof of this was when I took the train to Lausanne, Switzerland, where I was meeting a friend, Maggie. We were both visiting our amazing homeopath, Dr Senn, who has since cured me of a debilitating allergy to feathers and hay fever.

Maggie, who was taking the plane, and I left home at about the same time and she arrived in Lausanne only two hours before me, the tortoise who had taken the train. While I was relaxed after four glorious hours sitting in a delightful Swiss buffet gorging on *birchermüesli*, the exquisite Swiss national dish comprising of oats, nuts and fruit soaked in yogurt overnight, she was shaking with annoyance after endless holdups and having all her essential fluids confiscated.

'What sort of bomb would I make with my Dr Hauschka eucalyptus foot reviving deodorant?' she asked crossly.

No such ridiculous confiscations and security paranoia on the train.

But after saying all this, there are times when I still really want to fly. So I'm afraid I didn't wrestle too long with my eco-conscience when I had the chance to attend a Buddhist course in Japan.

By now I'd been practising Buddhism for a few years, and without sounding too evangelical — actually what the hell, I am going to sound evangelical — it had quietly become the most important thing in my life. This doesn't mean that other things were no longer important, but it had given me an understanding that underpinned and enhanced everything I did. The simple act of chanting *Nam-myoho-renge-kyo* and studying and attending meetings had gradually transformed me from a borderline depressive, easily swayed by life's vicissitudes, into a more secure and contented person. I hadn't magically ironed out life's problems, but I now had a tool to transform them into something positive.

When a friend recently said to me, 'You're a naturally happy person,' I really did a double take. The realisation that people see me as a happy person compared to the neurotic melancholic I used to be really makes me wish more people chanted too. It's free and it works.

For those of us brought up in the rationally inclined West it's hard to explain why it is effective. But you don't need to understand how electricity works to be able to switch on the lights; better therefore to chant and see the benefits than wait until you understand all the theory.

Buddhism is of course a very ancient philosophy with a number of basic tenets in common with all the major religions. One of these is 'Do as you would be done by'; that is, focus on kind thoughts, words and deeds as what you put out comes back (creating good or bad karma). It's not so outlandish. The happiest people I know are not the most beautiful or the richest but often the nicest. Goodness is its own reward.

In my favourite play, *A Man for All Seasons*, Sir Thomas More tries to persuade the materialistic Richard Rich to become a teacher instead of corrupting himself by becoming a self-serving courtier: 'But who would know if I was a good teacher?' Rich asks plaintively. 'You, your pupils ... God,' replies Sir Thomas. 'Not a bad public that.'

Buddhists do not believe in God — rather a more universal force of good — but we do believe that even if we do a good or bad thing and no one knows it, the universe (or in Sir Thomas's eyes, God) will recognise it and judge you on your deeds. An extra incentive then, for trying to do the right thing.

As my Buddhist practice had been so transformational I was dead keen to go to Japan, where this form of Buddhism began. I saw it as a pilgrimage, rather like a Catholic might go to Rome or a Muslim to Mecca. A powerful incentive for attending Buddhist courses is that they change you fundamentally and you always return with a deeper insight into a problem, which can be instrumental in solving it.

I've visited a small Buddhist centre in France which holds regular courses about fifteen times. Often on my return I've sorted out a seemingly intractable problem — usually to do with my family or a tortuous boyfriend situation. I've had an insight into my behaviour and seen there is usually something in me that must change before I can change the situation.

But visiting Japan is the big one. If things happen after a Badedas bath, things definitely happen after a tozan (a Buddhist pilgrimage) to Japan.

There's always room for improvement, of course, but I felt I was doing quite well. I had a harmonious relationship with my family most of the time, I loved writing my column — it was a dream come true — and I really felt I was a part of the whole green movement which I'm passionate about.

My relationship with my family, in particular my father, had improved vastly. It had changed so imperceptibly that I barely took note of the improvements, until one day I realised I'd lost all the resentments that had been festering; I no longer idealised him and felt healthily detached. I wondered why it had taken me so long.

In retrospect the coast was now finally clear for me to meet someone who would make me really happy — not a carbon copy of the father I had lost but still longed for. Those of us with an absent parent can spend our entire lives searching for him or her in our partners, but this desire is built on shaky foundations. Only when we make our foundations secure by coming to terms with the past can we create a stable and healthy future.

So life was pretty good. But it was about to become a lot better.

Chapter 9

A flirtation in the Far East

THEY say you find love when you're least looking for it, but I disagree — I hadn't been looking properly for over a year and I still hadn't met anyone. Sophocles wrote, 'Seek and ye shall find', and I concur. I mean if you want to find a new house you don't just wait for it to appear out of the blue — you register with an estate agent and keep your eyes open. So apart from a few hopeless yet agonising infatuations things had been all quiet on the romantic front. This respite from agonising romantic obsessions was soothing, if a bit dull, but I was very content and I'd got quite used to it.

I knew most of our motley gang of Buddhists travelling to Japan fairly well, but the one I knew the least, S — the wild man of Buddhism—I'd made of point of studiously avoiding for years. Five years previously we'd been attending the same course at the Buddhist centre in France and he'd begun talking to me in the bar. (Yes, we do have a bar — some Buddhists do drink. In fact I was practically teetotal until I began chanting, when I began to relax my fairly stringent dietary habits. Buddhism is all about finding a middle way — at least that's my excuse.)

So there I was, sipping my daily glass of Laurent-Perrier

Ultra Brut, favoured by supermodels as one of the lowest sugar champagnes on the market. (I should only drink delicious English fizz like Nyetimber but in the battle to reduce one's carbon emissions and one's figure, the latter occasionally takes priority.)

Anyway S, who was slightly the worse for wear (he hadn't yet found a middle way with booze) starts blathering on about something or other. I immediately thought, how boring, and slid back to the room I was sharing with my pal, Joyce, an air stewardess. An hour later someone starts banging on the door. I peered out of the window and recoiled in shock. It was him!

'Ugh! Joyce! Lock the door. It's that bloke from the bar! You know, the one wearing those tacky sunglasses!' Not that I'm a label snob but there are limits.

So we locked the door and put a chair against it for good measure. Based on this encounter I avoided talking to him for the next five years (not so easy as we lived in the same part of London and frequently attended the same meetings). Once I came out of a meeting and saw him walking in my direction and I sprinted past him mumbling, 'Sorry in a terrible rush!' to avoid any interaction.

But I revised my opinion slightly on the plane to Tokyo. I was sunk in gloom at the thought of possibly sharing a room and being removed from my daily me-me-me routines based entirely around my own myriad special needs, and desperately worried that my travel kettle might not work on the voltage (how could I face the morning without my flowery Earl Grey tea from Harrods made with my special net tea basket from Whittards?).

As a Buddhist you may well be thinking, why wasn't her mind on higher spiritual matters than tea? But tea is very important, and quite spiritual too if you think about all the ceremonies involving it. Besides, if you think I'm bad now you should have seen how I used to be.

Anyway, S nonchalantly strolled down the aisle and stopped for a chat and I thought, he's not as awful as I remembered. And he was very helpful about explaining the type of voltage in Japan. I held his eye for a moment longer than normal and he wandered off.

When you catch a man's eye and hold it, apparently it does something to their wiring — so he told me later — and for the next twelve days he was madly hot to trot. He carried my pointlessly enormous handbag about and flirted with me round the clock. He was someone with whom I could let off steam and have a good old un-Buddhist moan.

I knew he wasn't the man for me — he drank like a fish from dawn to dusk and earned a precarious living as a builder — but he treated me as an irresistible sex goddess and it was all tremendously boosting after the effete old Etonians who were my usual dating fodder. He pursued me like a heat-seeking missile and I was flattered by his constant attention. With his Jack-the-Lad confidence and quick flirty repartee he reminded me of Alfie, and Walker in *Dad's Army*, whilst he saw my snooty Lady Penelope persona as a challenge. He had unshakeable confidence — no matter how rude I was he always came back for more.

'Are you still takin' the gorgeous pills darlin'?' he would greet me first thing in the morning.

'Oh shut up and leave me alone,' I'd reply, batting my eyelashes furiously. I knew he was a drink-sodden himbo — albeit a very charming one — and I had no intention of falling for him. It was all just a bit of fun. Besides, though I wasn't really looking, I knew that if I did fall for someone he would be a tallish, darkish, German-speaking tycoon as per my perfect man list (it was fashionable at one time for single women to make a long list of their perfect man qualities). S wasn't any of these things, though he was fluent in flirting, if not in German.

So, although I was flattered I had no intention of pursuing our flirtation once we returned home. Our worlds were miles apart and all I wanted was a bit of fun and help with reactivating my dwindling pheromones.

One day we did have a bit of a tumble but we didn't go all the way because members of the party kept banging on the door at regular intervals — they seemed to be operating some sort of rota system. S had a reputation with the ladeez and they were determined to protect me from his advances.

Japan was as life changing for all of us as I'd hoped. The days raced by in a fascinating blur of ICE trains, visits to invigorating and joyous Buddhist schools, meetings, concerts and the chance to stay in the homes of Japanese Buddhists.

Japan is a dichotomy. On many levels it's very eco-friendly — spotless, efficient bullet trains reduce the need for cars and we sped around the country in a nanosecond. And like my grandparents, many householders have a reluctance to turn on the central heating unless icicles are growing in their ears. I don't think they do this to reduce their carbon emissions; it's more of a cultural thing — they simply don't seem to feel the cold.

One night I was billeted with a charming car tyre mogul and his family at his enormous, freezing house in Kyoto. As my extremities are like ice packs at the best of times, when we stayed the night anywhere I took the precaution of bringing along my trusty hot water bottle, and what a great luxury it proved to be. I always take one abroad, as they're like kettles — extremely difficult to find outside the UK, and when I have tried I've been fobbed off with enema bottles and all sorts. As I slipped into the kitchen to fill it before we went to bed it was quickly grabbed by the helpful lady of the house who then attempted to fill it with ice cubes.

S insisted it was because I looked so cold-blooded and that I must secretly be one of David Icke's lizards, part of the extra-terrestrial wicked ruling class who lay eggs of gold. I wish. Heat compensation came in the form of the delicious heated loo seats which are everywhere in Japan. They proved to be a great non-eco-comfort for my freezing lizard-like bottom. Not that this is any reference to cellulite you understand — before the trip I'd taken to massaging it with old coffee grounds. I read that Cindy Crawford does this and indeed my bottom is much improved.

But I was shocked to the core at the Japanese treatment of animals. One school showed us a video of an ex-pupil who was training a killer whale to perform pointless tricks in a swimming pool. Locking up wild creatures in solitary confinement was deemed to be a very good thing indeed. Japanese animals have no rights in the law — you don't even need a licence to experiment on them — thus terrible abuses are quite legal.

But before one points the finger too much, the Japanese eat far less meat than the supposed animal-loving Brits (although they are unfortunately eating more) and must be praised for managing to ingest so much cruelty-free tofu. We got mounds of this inedible quivering soya substance at every meal; I couldn't help but notice that it seemed to shudder even when there was no wind. But even this is better than the cold, slithery sushi that wobbles in your throat as you swallow it. Raw fish is full of parasites and they are often skinned alive to guarantee freshness. And I didn't touch the meat, as most animals are intensively farmed in even more barbaric conditions than in Europe. Oh dear, hands up who wants to have dinner with me? To be honest, I'm happiest of all with a piece of Gruyère cheese and an avocado. And yes, I am aware that Swiss cows are as flatulent as any other.

Fortunately, not eating much had resulted in a dramatic and exciting weight loss. Ironic then that I was breaking my trip home with a stop-over at the ritzy Chiva-Som health spa in Thailand. It was on the way back to the UK, so to speak, so I didn't feel quite so guilty about my dreadful carbon footprint.

On the last day I arrived at the airport after the rest of the team as my flight was much later. I was hoping to avoid saying goodbye to S, as his attentions were starting to drive me up the wall. It had been flattering but now I couldn't wait to escape. But to my chagrin, his flight hadn't yet been called and he spotted me across the marble concourse. His face lit up and he dashed over.

'I'll miss you darlin'.' He reached to hug me but I pulled away in irritation. 'I won't miss you at all,' I snapped back, seeking refuge in the duty-free shop.

But half an hour later I felt a burning desire to say goodbye properly and dashed out — but his flight had been called and he'd disappeared. My heart slumped; I so regretted my thoughtless goodbye and felt desperately lonely at the thought of jetting off into the unknown after such an uplifting and fascinating week.

I couldn't have chosen a lovelier place than Chiva-Som to be miserable though. It was also impressively eco-friendly. Water was conserved using rainwater harvesting, some of the energy came from renewable sources and most of the food was grown organically on site. But of course, if you have to fly to get to these *soi-disant* eco-friendly destinations you undo all your greenie points.

But despite the loveliness of my surroundings my mood

deteriorated even further. The place was full of honeymooning couples, my trusty laptop went dead when I spilt a tropical cocktail over it and I spent the week shuffling around in slippers feeling quite bereft. If only I hadn't been so foul to S — surely he'd never speak to me again. Who could blame him?

I couldn't wait to return home. It would be easier to endure my misery with all my things around me. On the flight back I read an article about how single-person households were destroying the planet with their selfish carbon-busting lifestyles and thought of S, back home in his squalid bachelor pad, chatting up some old trollop down his local pub, and sobbed.

But sometimes, just sometimes, life works out the way you hope …

Chapter 10

My love life lifts off

WHEN I arrived home, to my delight, amongst the pile of bills greeting me was a card from S. And I'd only been back a few hours when the phone rang. No surprises guessing who it was. To my relief he was still hot to trot and raced round to see me straight away.

Although it had been years since I'd dated anyone properly, I was surprised at how easily I got used to sharing my life again. I'd enjoyed being single for all the old chestnuts — time to myself, going to bed when I wanted … But I realised that in a good relationship you can still do this; you give up nothing and gain everything. It's wonderful having someone to share life's ups and downs with, who thinks you are fabulous first thing in the morning when even your own mother might admit you are looking a little rough around the edges.

But I had to lay down rules in the beginning just so there was no confusion. Chief among these was that I didn't do dinner parties and was very happy for him to go out as much as he wanted, but he mustn't expect me to go out with him. I had terrible memories of enforced socialising with my ex-husband's cronies and I had no wish to get into all of that again. Besides, I was too lazy to see enough of my own friends and rellos, let alone take on someone else's.

I eased myself into things quite slowly: for the first six months I negotiated at least three nights a week to myself, as to launch into one hundred per cent coupledom would have induced nervous exhaustion. Over the months I became more relaxed and able to share my personal space, but it didn't happen overnight. I did need to be trained up.

Fortunately, we're lucky to be living in a time when different forms of relationship can thrive because a conventional set-up of living together and getting married wouldn't work for us. Because we are both quite fiery it's just as well we keep our own separate flats. After a row S really needs his bachelor pit to stomp off to — we wouldn't have lasted two weeks without the cooling off chamber that is his untidy himbo hovel. Like many writers I crave solitude and have a tendency to 'call in sick' so I can have a night off to watch *Ashes to Ashes* DVDs and eat cheese. The hurly burly of the chaise longue appears to suit us better than the stability of the marital bed, at the time of writing anyway.

Besides, I strongly believe that living with your partner takes away much of the passion and you become more like brother and sister than lovers. As Esther Perel pointed out in her bestseller, *Mating in Captivity*, shacking up together is the quickest way to lose the romance and fizz in a relationship and turn your lover into a 'partner' (dreadful word). I think this would be heartbreaking.

However, separate homes presented a green conundrum. As I've mentioned, the big green story doing the rounds at this time was that single people (as if their lives weren't hard enough already) were major contributors to global warming. In my borough of Kensington and Chelsea, a staggering forty-eight per cent of us live alone, consuming nearly as much electricity and gas and creating nearly as much waste (think of the packaging for all those ready-made meals for one) as a couple or a family. These statistics are reflected across the nation: by 2020, forty per cent of UK households will be home to singletons. It's a growing trend worldwide which I'm afraid must remain one of my green holes.

The reason why living alone is a growing trend is because it's so pleasant. Unsustainable yes, but the chaotic thrills and spills of family life or flat share are not everyone's cup of tea. And what's not to like about enjoying the peace and quiet of your own mini fiefdom? Of course, I will happily live with someone when I'm decrepit and/or old, but in that case no one will want to live with me, so I shall probably end up employing some unfortunate factotum to mop my dribbling chin for a considerable sum.

This brings me back to the thorny problem of staff. My saintly cleaner, Norma Pipolotta was now fully trained up with my stringent green cleaning methods. She had become very fond of me, seeing me as a sort of surrogate daughter, and took a keen interest in my personal life. Mrs P loved nothing more than to discuss her personal problems and complain about her idle husband who was housebound due to a bad leg. She saw my flat as a refuge from him and her ungrateful middle-aged children who still lived at home. Listening to Mrs P's terrible tales of her ghastly offspring (combined age 120) was the most effective birth control method I knew — she could empty the nation's IVF clinics in a minute. As for the Pope, five minutes with Mrs P would convince him to provide free condoms along with communion. Employers who work from home are sucked guiltily into this emotional vortex with their cleaners — it's like being tuned into *EastEnders*, but less interesting and you can't switch it off.

But I had bad form when it came to staff intimacy problems, as I just wasn't authoritative enough to stop the unwanted confidences. Unless you start the way you intend to go on you're doomed for life.

I had become resigned to the unwelcome intimacy of our relationship but things took a sudden turn for the worse when I began dating S, and Mrs P took an instant dislike to him. I knew something was up, as she's usually an exemplary ironer but she kept burning his shirts 'by mistake'. I suspect she disapproved of me dating a builder as she had high hopes of me marrying a minor royal or mogul-type person.

So, I was quite relieved when she had to go home to the Philippines for a month and helpfully organised a replacement to cover for her. Due to bad organisation I'd also arranged cover too, so I was now in the fortunate position of having two cleaners who were a delight. They have no interest in my life, are politely indifferent to S and just crack on, manically burning fossil fuels and leaving as soon as they can. Best of all they speak no English so we communicate entirely in sign language. It is unbelievably restful.

However, it was hard work trying to explain my complex green house rules in sign language to these new cleaners who obviously think I'm slightly mad. Fifty years ago the way I live would seem quite normal. I turn off lights, conserve bath and washing up water which I scoop into buckets to water my window boxes. I hardly ever use the energy-gobbling tumble dryer (which I was now using as a handy clothes storage facility in the same manner as some girls use their ovens to store cashmere sweaters), which along with the kettle uses up the most energy in the average household. Food scraps go into a slop bucket (once an attractive china Crock-Pot until I threw it at S with the result that it's now very chipped and has half a lid). I usually wash clothes at 30°C (although I love a good boil wash as much as the next woman I'm trying to resist) and was having success with my Ecoballs, which are round plastic balls filled with tiny stones which replace the need for washing powder. I say *was* because one of the new cleaning ladies decided I needed to boil wash the sheets and used the Ecoballs, without realising that if they're used over 60°C they stop working and must be replaced.

Meanwhile, I've had to Sellotape the tumble dryer shut, frequently ferret around the communal bin area to make sure the regular rubbish is separated from the recyclables — Mrs A likes to bung everything in together. I'm all for the new electronic chips on bins to ensure we recycle, but fear my fines would be astronomical unless I continue my regular forays down to the bin room after her visits. Sometimes though, I get tired of explaining why the tumble dryer can't be used and about the separate bins and just let it happen.

However, I began to dread Mrs P's return, armed with hundreds of holiday snaps I knew she couldn't wait to share, along with the endless updates about her husband's bad leg, which according to a recent text update had taken a turn for the worse. The last straw was when S came home hot and dusty at 4.30 p.m. (builders start horrifically early so clocking off at this time isn't a sign of idleness) and she asked sarcastically, 'Not working again today, S?'

This was the limit and I had to 'let her go'. This was predictably awful but an enormous relief. I tried to save her pride by explaining I was about to embark on the marathon building work so I wouldn't need a cleaner for months and that I couldn't possibly expect her to keep my days free.

Mrs P's snobbish attitude made me realise that the class system is unfortunately alive and well in the UK — while cross-race marriages are now the norm, cross-class ones are still quite rare. My relationship with S was exposing all sorts of prejudices and preconceptions I thought had expired after the Lady Chatterley trial in 1961 and it was the most unlikely people who disapproved. The people whose opinion mattered the most, like my family, had practically given up hope I would ever date again and were just hugely relieved I'd found anyone at all. Their only requirement was that S made me happy; they couldn't give a fig about his background.

But relationships are statistically happiest when we choose a partner from the same background, and I can see why this is. It may mean you have the same attitude to money, education and a similar upbringing and experiences, which is a great help. However, I am a class hybrid — with one grandfather a baronet and the other a cockney, my parents hailed from opposite ends of the spectrum — so no one is more aware than me of the pitfalls of cross-class marriage. But it does make me more open minded about dating people from all backgrounds — besides it's so hard to find someone you fancy who fancies you back at the best of times, if you start limiting yourself to one class you're narrowing down the field even further.

As far as I'm concerned, working class men make the best boyfriends. It's just so much easier being with a man who isn't caught up in middle class mores. The upper classes and the working classes are infinitely preferable to the insecure middles who use massive amounts of energy trying to keep up with everyone else. At the top and the bottom they do what they want, when they want and are far less worried about the good opinion of others.

For example, the middle classes are obsessed about eating at a socially acceptable time for dinner. They'd as soon eat dinner at 6 p.m. than cut off their arm. The upper classes eat when they're hungry and the working classes usually eat very early in the evening. This suits me as I'm too impatient and greedy to wait for the fashionably late 9 p.m., which is the socially acceptable dining hour for the smarty set. Besides, eating late is bad for the figure — this is why Sloanes are so plump.

Meanwhile, upper class men are often full of neuroses about women, escaping to male-only institutions and only able to relax with them when tanked up with booze. They hide their shyness behind charming but pointless chivalrous rituals — bobbing up and down like lifebuoys when a lady leaves and returns to the room, opening car doors and walking on the outside of pavements — and yet they are unable to do anything really useful, like change a wheel or find the stopcock in the middle of the night when there is a leak.

Dating blue-blooded men dooms one to a life of fancy restaurants, dinner parties (even more unbearable and tedious than the theatre) glitzy parties and many tortuous forms of culture including ballet (ballet! I'd rather endure water torture over a bunch of prancing tutu-wearing monkeys any day of the week). And as for charity balls where one coughs up a fortune to eat rubber chicken and dance to some tinny band in the company of braying Tories and aspirational merchant bankers — well I'd rather pay not to attend. I've lucked out with S, who is blissfully low maintenance socially and whose idea of a good night out is playing snooker down the pub, with girlfriends firmly discouraged. Nights in mean dinner in front of the telly at 6.30 p.m. Who could ask for more?

Perhaps I'm tapping into a trend. As men become alarmingly metrosexual (weeping at football matches, growing moobs and carrying 'man bags'), women secretly yearn for a thuggish but practical Grant Mitchell-type as opposed to the cute-faced and floppy-haired Hugh Grant figure (high earning but can't change a fuse).

Chapter 11

Tempted by a telecommunications tycoon

IT'S ALL very well living a green life when you're single, but what to do if your inamorato doesn't share your desire to go green? Since I've been coupled up, I've realised going green gives couples limitless scope for round-the-clock bickering. It was one thing training up my cleaning ladies, but S represented a whole new strata of green worrydom.

'Who do you think we are?' I would screech as he threw tea leaves down the waste disposal instead of into a china pot, the correct depository for such detritus, 'the Rockefellers?' My worms love tea leaves — I think the caffeine stimulates them. Besides, there's money in compost these days.

In the heady early days of our romance he created further shockwaves by shoving bottles into the recycling bag with their lids on and envelopes into the paper recycling bag without removing the plastic window (these can usually be recycled now but back then was a definite no-no).

He's much better now, but my goodness, the early days were a challenge! But there is still one terrible flashpoint, and that's travel. S's idea of a cracking holiday is to go on Teletext and find the cheapest bargain hot hols he can find. His last holiday without me involved a 3 a.m. wake-up and a hideous Ryanair flight to Tunisia to stay at a vast hotel complex. There he took up with a crowd of Mancunians and got so drunk on his last night they shaved off his eyebrows and half his hair. I'm weaning myself off flying and attempting to find lovely resorts in France and Switzerland we can reach by train, but still S tempts me with his 'bargains'. I've taken to reading out this eloquent explanation of the effects of our holiday flights on Greenland's Inuit people, written by their leader, Aqqaluk Lynge:

> You may say that the expansion of London Stansted airport will play only a small part in increasing climate change, but everyone can say that about almost everything they do. It is an excuse for doing nothing. The result of that attitude would be catastrophic.
>
> The serious consequences affecting my people today will affect your people tomorrow. Most flights from Stansted are not for an important purpose. They are mostly for holidays and leisure. Is it too much to ask for some moderation for the sake of my people today and your people tomorrow? For the sake also of our wildlife and everything else in the world's precious and fragile environment that is more important than holiday flights.
>
> The Inuit are experiencing first-hand the adverse effects of climate change. We are on the frontline of globalisation. Discussion of climate change frequently tends to focus on political, economic and technical issues rather than human impacts and consequences. I want to alert you to the impacts that Inuit and other northerners are already experiencing as a result of human-induced climate change, and to the dramatic impacts and social and cultural dislocation we face in coming years.
>
> For generations, Inuit have observed the environment and

have accurately predicted weather, enabling us to travel safely on the sea-ice to hunt seals, whales, walrus, and polar bears. We don't hunt for sport or recreation. Hunters put food on the table. You go to the supermarket; we go on the sea-ice. When we can no longer hunt on the sea-ice, we will no longer exist as a people. Already hunters are telling us the sea-ice is unpredictable in many places and they are not always sure of dealing with the different ice we see today.

Traditional hunting grounds of ice floes, in some cases, have disappeared. And they tell us that some hunting areas are impossible to get to because of eroding shorelines. Talk to hunters across the north and they will tell you the same story: the weather is increasingly unpredictable. The look and feel of the land is different. The sea-ice is changing.

Climate change is not just a theory to us in the Arctic; it is a stark and dangerous reality. Human-induced climate change is undermining the ecosystem upon which Inuit depend for their physical and cultural survival. Think about that for a moment. Emissions of greenhouse gases from planes, cars and factories threatens our ability far to the north to live in harmony with a fragile, vulnerable, and sensitive environment.

Some might dismiss our concerns, saying: 'The Arctic is far away and few people live there.' That would be immensely short-sighted, as well as callous.

The Arctic is of vital importance in the global debate on how to deal with climate change. That's because the Arctic is the barometer of the globe's environmental health. You can take the pulse of the world in the Arctic. Inuit, the people who live farther north than anyone else, are the canary in the global coal mine.

By 2070 to 2090, year-round sea-ice will be limited to a small portion of the Arctic Ocean around the North Pole. The rest of the Arctic will be ice-free in summer. Polar bears, *walrus, ringed seals, and other species of seals are projected to virtually disappear. Our ecosystem will be transformed, with tragic results. Where will we go then for our food? What then will become of the Inuit? Climate change in the Arctic is not just an environmental issue with unwelcome economic consequences. It is a matter of individual and cultural survival. It is a human issue. The Arctic is our home and homeland.*

What can Inuit — only 155,000 of us — do about this global situation? We are not asking the world to take a backward economic step. All we are asking is that our neighbours in the south greatly reduce their emissions of greenhouse gases. This does not need big sacrifices, but it will need some change in people's lifestyles. Is that plane trip really necessary?

This is written so beautifully and is so very emotive, how can one ever look an aeroplane in the face again? S agrees with me at the time but then returns the next day with another amazing deal. As a consequence we rarely end up going anywhere together.

Besides, any holiday I do manage to organise goes terribly wrong. Last summer I arranged a trip to the Scilly Isles. We like a good train journey — just as well, as it is six hours to Penzance, followed by a three-hour ferry trip to the isles. We broke the journey at Jean Shrimpton's much lauded hotel in Penzance and then took a ferry to the Scillies. Hell's Bay, on the tiny island of Bryer, was gorgeous; I loved it but it was breathtakingly expensive. Our weekend ended up costing us £1,200 each and all the shuffling around on trains and ferries was exhausting. Hardly value for money when S informs me his pal 'stressed out Dave the plasterer' just paid five hundred quid for fourteen nights in a five-star hotel in Mexico, including all he could eat and drink.

He has forbidden me from organising our trips from now

on, insisting I'm the Imelda Marcos of holiday planning. No wonder he prefers to find his holidays on Teletext. They may be hideous and involve drunken scalpings, but they're hot and cheap.

It's so hard to resist temptation. We could have stayed a week at the Kahala Mandarin Oriental in Hawaii for the same price. Business class flights would have been a bargain £200 from Joyce, the air stewardess, who before my no-go-fly-policy frequently furnished me with bargain biz flights round the world.

See how the devil tempts you? I need the Bishop of London, he of the wonderful 'flying is a symptom of sin' speech on speed-dial for instant guidance. Some people got quite self-righteous about this speech, as we live in an age where the rights of the individual are seen as more important than the collective good. But I think it was very brave of him to take a stance that politicians are too lily-livered to make.

But even the Bishop might be hard pressed to persuade anyone to holiday at home when the food and weather is so variable and the trains, ferries and hotels often ruinously expensive. Plus, so many hotels have carpets in the bathrooms — it's so unhygienic. It won't stop me holidaying in Britain because I know there are well-priced glorious hotels. The trouble is one needs the skill of Sherlock Holmes to track them down.

Unfortunately no good deed goes unpunished and my attempts at eco-friendly holidaying had repercussions. For, when I castigated the perils of holidaying in 'rip off Britain' in my column, I was stunned to receive a rabid green ink email from Janet Street-Porter:

I read your column and thought it was sour drivel. Shame

you didn't read the piece I wrote about St Ives for the Sat travel section before making your feeble plans. If you want to fly on a cheap flight to Mexico for a package deal holiday for £500 then don't call yourself a Green Goddess.

It was like being savaged by a national institution! I wrote back concluding: 'Despite my poorly researched trip I will persevere and consider your recommendations from now on, if nothing else but to allow you to save some ire for Hitler and Stalin.'

She responded: 'My ire is justified because I don't call myself any kind of goddess!'

Boom boom!

My next trip was by myself and more successful. I visit the wonderful Mayr clinic in Austria twice a year and instead of flying to Innsbruck now take a sleeper train which is far more of an adventure. The Mayr cure is popular with middle class Brits, who seem particularly keen on bowel cures, and the *Daily Mail*, which regularly sends incognito reporters to write 'hilarious' (well, they think so) reports on some of the more outré treatments.

Inmates spend much of the day gathered around the 'tea station' — a large area dispensing all manner of foul-tasting bowel-cleansing herbal brews — for a good moan. On my last visit I got talking to Clement Freud who is a great fan of the place.

'And what does your boyfriend do?' he enquired politely.

'He's a builder,' I explained.

'Ah.' Long pause. 'Did you find him in the Yellow Pages?'

He then launched into a story about a well-known soap star who whenever she was single reached for her Yellow Pages and organised for a series of quotes from builders, plasterers and plumbers, several of whom she went on to form lasting relationships with. Nobody seems to use the Yellow Pages any more but maybe it should stage a comeback as a lonely hearts directory.

Soon after this I was invited to lunch with a handsome mobile phone tycoon, as he wanted to pick my brains about setting up a green website. I'd met him at a party some while before and had been very impressed by his enthusiasm to green up his life and his business — he'd just installed solar panels on his country house.

'People want to be green,' he'd asserted, 'but they don't know where to start as it seems so complicated. I want this website to make it easier for them.'

I'd agreed with him but later changed my mind. If people are intelligent enough to sort out a mortgage, find a house they can just about afford, a school for their child and research and book cheap holidays on the internet, surely the need to switch off lights, turn the heating down and refuse plastic bags can't be too complicated to grasp?

I think this apathy must be because in the UK we've been largely protected from the growing crisis of global warming. If we lived in a part of the world drastically affected — like the islands of Tuvalu, which are sinking so fast its inhabitants are being relocated to New Zealand, or Australia, facing an ongoing drought, or Bangladesh, at a constant risk of flooding — perhaps we would have more incentive to change our ways.

But so far most Brits, having put up with centuries of cold and rain, rather like the thought of global warming. Hot summers, lemon trees in the garden and English wine? Bring it on. But as we are seeing with floods, storms and changeable summers, we're not just facing global warming but extreme climate instability as well. But until those of us in the developed world can perceive the threat with our own eyes I fear that we won't change our behaviour in time to avert a catastrophe. Not enough people are public-spirited enough to make the necessary steps to reduce emissions, and yet when the threat is visible — for example, when Hitler threatened our borders in 1939 — the majority of the population complied with blackouts, belt tightening and rationing for the common good.

Global warming seems a far more nebulous danger which is still not really perceived as much of a threat at all. If London is flooded and tornados wipe out our cities perhaps things will really change, but by then it may be too late anyway. But looking on the bright side, even if the human race is annihilated the planet will still survive and adapt — even if the only things that can survive at first are rats and cockroaches.

I was also looking forward to lunch with the telecoms tycoon because S and I were going through a rocky patch. The very things that attracted me to him, his occasional fecklessness, the laid back and relaxed attitude to life, were the things that drove me up the wall too. And although I'm not hugely materialistic — I no longer have a desire to own a car, more clothes or a second home, and fancy nights out leave me cold — there were times when I secretly wondered what it must be like to be with a man who could live his life without financial constraints.

While these days it's common for women to earn more than men that doesn't mean that either side really likes it very much. So a part of me was thinking a green-minded magnate might be just what the doctor ordered.

But I was wrong.

For a start the mobile mogul was businesslike and certainly not flirtatious. Most commendable! And then he said something which made a light bulb go off in my head and I realised a tycoon — even an apparently green one — was not for me.

'It's nice having a girlfriend,' he mused, 'because then you have someone to organise a social life and dinner parties for you.'

I cringed. Dinner parties! I couldn't be bothered to feed my own friends, let alone someone else's. This would be the hideous reality of dating a business mogul — devoting yourself to their happiness and subjugating your own 'special needs' for their comfort. What sort of life would that be?

If I'm honest I knew this already. My father is a tycoon of sorts, and while I am his greatest fan I have observed that his girlfriend is fully employed tending to his special needs. In fact, with a magnate in the house you will never be in control of your television remote control again — remote will indeed be the word for it. *Desperate Housewives* will be abandoned for endless sports programmes and you will be chained to the kitchen cooking enormous man-style meals (delicious easy-to-assemble girl's food — stuff like goat's cheese, sheep's yogurt and avocado sprinkled with flax seeds, rounded off with a bar of dark chocolate — won't cut the mustard). There was no way I was cut out to be tycoon totty. If anyone was going to be tended it was going to be *moi* thank you very much.

S might not have money but he was funny, sexy, kind and he treated me like a goddess. Despite our rows, or maybe because of them, the chemistry between us sizzled. He was also marvellously handy round the house and fixed things without being asked. He came with me to environmental building exhibitions where we both got (quite) excited about hemp bricks. He peed on the compost heap. Would a mobile mogul do that? I don't think so. Besides, how many men would put up with my insatiable desire for solitude, my independence and my obsession with unpasteurised cheese? We were a great team.

It was quite ironic that for years I'd believed only a wealthy, tall, dark and handsome type would be right for me — I'd even written down these qualities on my 'perfect man list' years ago — but I'd ended up with someone diametrically opposed to what I thought I wanted. Thank goodness I'd finally seen sense.

Whilst wealth and social connections are wonderful things they are just icing on the cake — and I was beginning to realise it was the cake, not the icing, that mattered. Character and personality are more important than a man's bank balance (although having all three would, of course, be perfection). The trouble is that so many women, myself included, are indoctrinated by the eternal and destructive fantasy of being rescued.

From childhood we are conditioned by fairytales of helpless princesses being rescued by handsome princes, while in adulthood movies like *Pretty Woman* and *Sex in the City* do the same thing by pandering to our secret dreams of being swept off our feet by a stronger, richer, alpha male like Mr Big or Richard Gere. In your dreams, girls! It is a universal truth that men who are 'good on paper' just don't live up to the promise in the flesh. Why aren't girls taught essential facts like this in schools, along with how to wire a plug?

When the *Sex in the City* TV series first hit our screens in the late 1990s, like many of us I thought the gorgeous, powerful but ultimately unavailable Mr Big was the ideal man. But he and all those other romantic leads are nothing more than characters in a fantasy. It's a great disappointment that

Carrie ends up with a fantasy Mr Big in the film — in the real world of course he would have ditched Carrie and ended up with a series of 18-year-old Russian models. But maddeningly the myth is thus perpetuated for another generation ...

And so my lunch with the phone tycoon gave me plenty of food for thought and reiterated one of my favourite Buddhist texts written in the thirteenth century by Buddhist monk, Nichiren Daishonin, whose teachings members of SGI follow: 'More valuable than treasures in a storehouse are the treasures of the body, and the treasures of the heart are the most valuable of all. From the time you read this letter on, strive to acquire the treasures of the heart!'

Thank goodness it just took a quick lunch to shake me up.

And besides, a mobile phone magnate would be no good for me as I'd been researching the debilitating effects of 'electromagnetic smog' caused by mobile phones, phone masts and Wi-Fi, about which there are mounting fears — heavily discounted, obviously, by those in the telecommunications business.

'There's no evidence mobile phones cause any health problems at all,' he had asserted confidently over lunch.

But I knew differently. A few months back I'd installed Wi-Fi at home, which had enabled me to log on to the internet anywhere in my flat without the need for extra wires. It was wonderful, but as I soon discovered, it was to have a terrible effect on my health ...

Chapter 12

Electrosmog shock

IT ACTUALLY took several months before I connected the installation of my Wi-Fi with various health problems that had begun to manifest. I'd noticed a real drop in my energy levels and was feeling generally out of sorts. Usually a good sleeper I'd suddenly begun waking up early in the morning and finding myself unable to go back to sleep. It wasn't only me that was drooping. My once lush plants had lost their lustre too. Ridiculous, considering how well I look after myself — and my plants. As you may have gathered I'm pretty well doctored. At one time I probably consulted more doctors than Woody Allen, who has separate screenings of his movies for his, and my frequent health checks ruled out any serious malady.

But despite my knowledge I couldn't work out why I felt so tired. When at a loss for a diagnosis I visit Dr Black, a naturopath and douser who never fails to get to the root of any health problem. It may sound unorthodox but who cares if it works — and her clientele, ranging from royals, celebrities and hypochondriacs like me, would be quite lost without her.

She is so effective I now use her as a one-stop shop and

thanks to her I've cut down on many treatments and vitamins that I really didn't need. She's saved me a fortune.

Dr Black insisted my problem was caused by 'electromagnetic smog' in my flat. She explained that our dependence on office and communications equipment (for example, mobile phones and the masts needed to power them, microwaves, computers and electrical equipment) also emit frequencies which can have a detrimental effect on our well-being, especially if we are rundown or our immune system is compromised in some way.

So I immediately turned off my wireless network and replaced it with broadband. Although it was convenient being able to access emails and the internet all over the flat without resorting to wires and plugs, if returning to broadband meant improving my energy levels it would be a small price to pay.

S paid lip service to my concerns and there was much nodding in agreement as I waffled on while he was doing the crossword, but he obviously hadn't been listening to a word I said because the next time he tried to access his emails on the laptop he kept at my place he got into a terrible strop when he couldn't log on. I tried unsuccessfully to blind him with science.

'Did you know', I began bossily, reading from my *Electrosmog* newsletter, 'that the pioneer in the field of bioelectromagnetics, Dr Robert O. Becker, who wrote the book, *The Body Electric* and was twice nominated for the Nobel Prize, claims that electromagnetic pollution is the greatest threat to our environment, greater even than global warming?'

But it cut no ice. 'I need to get on lastminute.com to check out some good deals,' he huffed. 'I'm fed up with this bloody weather — if I don't get some sun soon I'll go completely mad.'

I stomped off. Honestly, the man is completely oblivious to the plight of the Inuits as well as to the really terrible electromagnetic threat that was suffocating us all. But I stuck to my guns and kept the Wi-Fi off, which meant we were limited to just one computer which is attached to the phone line. As you might imagine there were fearful tussles when we wanted to check our emails at the same time, a problem which at the time of writing has still not been satisfactorily resolved. To lessen electromagnetic exposure I've taken a few precautions which I believe have helped. When I use my mobile I now use a headset which delivers sound through an air-filled wireless tube (similar to a doctor's stethoscope but much smaller so you don't get mistaken for a doctor on call).

I also use an electromagnetic field protection unit which is plugged in at home. This was created after years of research by scientist and homeopath Gary Johnson, a leader in the field of electromagnetic research. The unit claims to offer unlimited protection from any negative electromagnetic emissions within a seven hundred metre radius and soon after starting to use it I noticed an improvement in my energy levels and I sleep much better. Even my plants perked up.

When I wrote an article in *The Independent* asking for more caution and research to be done before Wi-Fi was rolled out with impunity across the land I was stunned to receive at least fifty abusive emails from angry men castigating me for my scientific ineptitude. Many were livid that a layman had had the temerity to enter the Wi-Fi debate.

'Young lady!' boomed one pompous fellow, 'before you put your fingers to the keyboard again do your research.'

Crikey!

The letters editor of *The Independent* was in such a state about the amount of vitriolic mail spewing into the letters pages he insisted I go in to the office to look at them. He was in such a panic I thought he might offer me police protection, which I was all for — an armed guard would at least protect me from a crazed Albanian lesbian who'd been harassing me by text and email for six years, as well as ensuring my car wasn't broken into again. (Yes, I still had a car, though in my defence I rarely used it, as to do so would lose my coveted parking space near my house — impossible to regain once lost.)

'It's not just all these letters!' the letters editor huffed, 'but Ben Goldacre has had a go at you in the Bad Science column in the *Guardian*!'

Rushing out to buy the *Guardian* I was hugely relieved to read the following: 'Julia Stephenson, the charming heiress to a beef fortune who lives in Chelsea …'

Stop right there! I knew it wasn't going to get any better than that so I put the paper down immediately. Well, that's a lie actually, but I could easily bear the attack on my Wi-Fi views because of the charming heiress bit. How fragile is the human ego!

A few months later when all this had died down I signed up to Facebook one evening when I'd had a few drinks and in a flurry of now-regretted enthusiasm, as you do, whizzed around the site signing up everyone I knew (and some I didn't) as a friend. One of these was Ben and he replied with a jolly note. So now I suppose we are frenemies. I guess it is a good thing that one can be fighting things out in the press while at the same time rising above it in cyberspace (not Wi-Fi enabled, of course).

In retrospect, if hard times don't kill you they make you stronger but at the time the whole situation was desperately upsetting. The abuse seemed out of all proportion to my actions — I was only counselling caution and was one of many commentators saying the same thing.

The trouble is there are so many vested interests involved in this issue and many people stood to lose out, particularly those involved in the telecommunications business if there was a sudden worldwide Wi-Fi switch-off.

A friend reassured me that when you stick your head above the parapet you have to take the knocks. He insisted that 'all publicity is good publicity as long as they spell your name right!' But many of my correspondents had been calling me 'Juliet' (presumably mixing me up with Juliet Stevenson, the redoubtable actress), so this just plunged me into an even greater gloom.

However, it was good to get the issue out there and discussed more widely. I received many emails from people who were suffering hugely from electromagnetic sensitivity. They were constantly frustrated that their concerns were so quickly dismissed and that big business held sway every time over the concerns of those without a voice, influence or money.

The episode left me much thicker skinned. Now when I write something controversial I think, bring it on.

Chapter 13

Cheese is good for you

SOME months after the Wi-Fi debacle I found myself completely incapacitated by hay fever triggered by pollen, dust and feathers. It caught me by surprise, as I'd never suffered from allergies before.

I was told it might have been brought on by the stress of my trial by Wi-Fi but I suspected differently. For sure it must be the final revenge of my first husband. He had been allergic to cats and feathers but I had always dismissed his sneezing and told him to get a grip. How I wish I had been more sympathetic! Talk about bad karma — my chicken (feathers) had really come home to roost.

I consulted all my doctors and tried every lotion, potion and pill I could get my hands on. Nothing worked and I got worse and worse. Fortunately my pal Maggie, who is as well doctored as me and is discovering extraordinary new practitioners all the time, suggested I visit Dr Senn, her Swiss homeopath.

Dr Senn, she explained, specialises in removing the toxic effects of inoculations from our body. A side effect of all the jabs we have is a suppression of immunity which can block energy pathways and manifest itself in allergies, health problems and depressing lingering illnesses like glandular fever and ME.

Indeed hay fever, eczema and allergies to common food stuffs like peanuts are on the increase, especially in children, and she attributes this to the increasing number of inoculations we receive at a very young age.

Always eager to add a new physician to my ever-expanding doctor roster I immediately rang Dr Senn for an appointment. But this is not a straightforward procedure. You call, leave a message and at some stage she will call you back, usually about at about 8 a.m. (an excruciating 7 a.m. UK time). She won't use your answer machine, so if you're desperate to see her you must keep your phone under your pillow and close to your bosom at all times so you don't miss her call. She's not keen on speaking English either (although she speaks it fluently) so these long-distance arrangements must be made in my painful schoolgirl French.

It's always good to have an excuse to visit Switzerland, a country of sparkling cities, ravishing scenery and one of the highest recycling rates in Europe. The country is full of men in electric vehicles manically mopping the streets and it is just the place to come for a holiday if you have a dust allergy. Yet for some unfathomable reason people say the country is boring. They have obviously never experienced the joy that is a Swiss train or witnessed the efficacy of the country's rubbish taxes at close hand. Not only do supermarkets charge for plastic bags, with the result that people bring their own, but in most parts of Switzerland throwing away rubbish costs money. Each garbage bag has to have a sticker on it, and each sticker costs at least one euro. So the less you throw out, the less you pay. No sticker? Then the refuse will be left outside your house to rot.

When I worked as a chalet girl in Switzerland we didn't

want to waste our meagre budget on buying rubbish bags so we'd cunningly package our waste into tiny parcels and deposit them in public bins late at night when Le Pub had shut. Several girls got into hot water when their rubbish was traced back to them because they'd discarded items containing personal information and been traced by the rubbish gendarmerie whose job it was to comb through the nation's refuse.

I was very strict with my chalet guests (or punters as they were affectionately known behind their backs). When I caught one of them sneakily putting a glass bottle into the bin I had a fit. I could get fifty cents per bottle — enough to feed a punter for a week in those days. 'What d'you think we are, made of money?' I spluttered, retrieving it immediately. Stupid punters. I didn't stay in that job long I can tell you, though it did provide enough material for my second novel, a gripping account of an immensely bossy vegan chalet girl who runs off with a spare car parts tycoon called Max (such a manly name!) who drove a Porsche — yes, a Porsche, I'm afraid I wasn't very enlightened in those days.

Max was inspired by a misalliance with a bald South African Porsche driving businessman, a big wheel in car accessories, who I dated for a year during which time he took me to various lovely places but never laid a finger on me. I never found out why he didn't want to have sex — if he hadn't fancied me why did he bother with all the fancy restaurants and exotic trips? Perhaps he was gay and 'in denial'? I'd love to know what the reason was; if I ever bump into him in the street I shall be sure to ask.

Other girlfriends have reported similar experiences, so I think some men, like women, are just not interested in sex, but this can be a bit pulverising for women as men are meant to be up for it all the time. One friend, Anne, confided she'd had the same experience with a similar tycoony chap, who'd confessed after six months of no sex that he used 'sex as a weapon' with his girlfriends. 'Some weapon,' she'd replied bitterly.

Another admitted her on-off boyfriend had wooed her for a year but that he 'respected her too much' for 'full intimacy' as he put it, though apparently 'non-penetrative sex' (his phrase again) was OK. What's going on? Is this lack of desire linked to oestrogens in the tap water and is it related to the alarming increase of man boobs? Moobs never used to exist but since being spotted on Jack Nicolson in 2006 now seem to be flopping about everywhere. Regarding the libido problems, according to confidences amongst my friends, it seems to be mainly mogulish types who seem to be afflicted; men with no money appear to be as libidinous as ever. Not that I'm experienced enough in these matters to make generalisations, you understand. Fortunately the situation was happily put to rights in my novel where Max (you know who you are!) was thrillingly hot to trot.

Anyway, I digress. After a fascinating consultation with Dr Senn (who gave me various pills and powders to cure me of my allergies to dust and *la plume* — these things sound so much better in French) I hopped on the train to visit Jane, a friend who was bravely doing up a wreck of a chalet in Gstaad. Renovating is the best time to install green features so I was keen to talk her into installing solar panels, insulation and a 'living' moss roof — I'd even brought along some mini-samples of eco-friendly paints to tempt her with.

But before I could say 'George Monbiot' she'd dragged me up to a distant glacier to do some late spring skiing. You'd think being a veteran chalet girl I might be able to ski to a competent level. *Au contraire*, I'm completely rubbish. I can understand damaging my body for something enjoyable like biodynamic champagne drinking, but for skiing? But Jane's a forceful girl and she had hired a ski guide so reluctantly I joined her.

As we slithered over the glistening sun-drenched slopes with guide Bruno my heart sank with the pointlessness of it all. We would take interminable cold ski lifts up mountains and then ski down them in a few frightening minutes. Why were we wasting our energy in this way? By 10 a.m., delirious with boredom, I insisted we break for an early lunch and fell ravenously upon a plate of Hobelkase, a delicious local cheese.

Bruno explained that his and many other local families belonged to the milk cooperative which produced it. The whole operation was run by a mysterious sounding fellow called Hanspeter Reust, a sort of James Bond of Swiss cheese-making, operating from a bunker built into the mountains. The entrepreneurial son of local cheese makers, he'd built up a mini-cheese empire and now sold his fromage all over the world.

Longing for an excuse to get off games I begged Bruno to give him a ring and ask if he'd like to be interviewed for a 'prestigious English newspaper'.

'Ahh, the *Daily Express*?' enquired Bruno as he dialled. He'd been a ski guide to a bunch of *Express* journalists a week ago and I think it was the only British paper he'd ever heard of.

'Certainly not!' I retorted. The *Express* is a conundrum. At the time of writing it sells about 750,000 copies every day yet I've never met anyone who claims to read it, but judging by these figures someone must. In fact it's highly likely you count a secret *Express* reader amongst your closest friends. It's the complete opposite of *The Independent* which everybody claims to read but nobody really does, as it only sells 153,000 copies a day, and is always the last paper to get pinched in Starbucks. It's a bit like the Barbara Cartland phenomenon. She's sold over a billion books, but have you ever seen anyone actually buy or read one? Most bookshops don't even sell them — where on earth can they all have gone?

Bruno made me an appointment with Hanspeter that afternoon so with some relief I slid back to the village (mainly on my bottom as I didn't want to take any risks with my precious knees) to track him down at the Molkerei shop, a glorious cornucopia of local dairy produce which he owns in Gstaad high street.

Hanspeter was a real charmer. Tall and weathered, he wore a Moroccan hat and was boiling over with enthusiasm for the exciting world of *le fromage*. After showing me around his shop he whisked me to his secret subterranean cheese HQ, an underground tardis carved deep into a deserted hillside.

Pressing a gadget, the doors swung open and I followed him down a steep ladder into the bowels of the earth. The door slammed behind us. Opera music blared, a white crystal shimmered in the middle of the room and the walls were lined with hundreds of round cheeses. The air was pungent, rich and sweet.

As we stood sipping delicious Swiss wine and sampling his cheese I looked at his handsome weathered face and thought with a shiver of alarm that here I was in this secret cheese bunker in the middle of nowhere with a perfect stranger! Anything could happen — I was in a really quite vulnerable situation, I thought hopefully, as a frisson of excitement and danger shot through me.

As the music echoed around the stone chamber and the crystal glistened, Hans explained the philosophy behind his business. This part of Switzerland, the Saanenland, is famous not just for its ritzy ski area but for producing wonderful food too. It's an area of staggering natural beauty, with its pure soil, sparkling air, sun and wind producing the finest milk in Switzerland. He pays local farmers a premium so they can afford to farm traditionally, milking by hand and feeding the cows on wild meadow grasses which are dried for the winter, instead of silage which results in a poorer tasting cheese.

Hans passionately believes that eating food from this region gives us good health and a lightness of spirit. We are what we eat, and it's a lovely thought that by eating the produce of the Saanenland we too can be imbued with its lushness, calm and peace.

The cheeses in the bunker were all unpasteurised. Hans explained this meant they were still alive and bursting with health-giving microorganisms that hadn't been killed off by the intense heat process and were therefore receptive to wonderful music and the energy created from the huge white crystal. You may scoff, but he must have been doing something right as his fromage is delicious and is sold from Geneva to Singapore.

It was a lovely interlude and with some regret I was released from the bunker, armed with samples, to return to the ravages of Jane's semi-done-up chalet and the real world.

The Swiss are fortunate in that they are still connected to their farmers and the provenance of their food in a way that many of us Brits no longer are, although this is changing speedily thanks to the growing trend of fabulous farmers markets and the interest in regional produce. Eating local food connects us with our countryside in a way that going into the supermarket and buying over-packaged shrink-wrapped food of unknown provenance never can.

You may wonder what the long suffering S thought of me gallivanting around Europe eating cheese with Moroccan-hatted men in caves — well, not a lot it must be said. In my case absence certainly didn't make my heart grow fonder and our daily phone calls seemed stilted and dull. When I called he was usually miserably plumbing in a sink or tiling a bathroom and we didn't have very much to talk about. With the geographical and emotional distance between us I was again riddled with doubts about our relationship.

Things soon improved when on my return to London he was waiting outside the Eurostar terminal to greet me. As we bickered about whether to take the bus (his choice) or a cab (mine) home (I reasoned that having sat on a train all sodding day I couldn't face any more public transport, global warming or no), I squeezed his arm, inhaled his smell and thought how good it was to be home.

How I wished we'd stayed there.

For soon afterwards, to make up for my holiday (or working trip as I preferred to call it) by myself, we decided to trip off by train for a five-day mini-break. At a friend's party we'd met a woman who rented out her apartment in the South of France and she painted such a glorious picture of the place we couldn't resist. It would be so lovely to have some 'quality' time together.

But a terrible shock awaited us. Instead of a spacious apartment we found ourselves in a shoebox with a tiny dribbling shower which was accessed by standing on the toilet. No refuge would be found in sleep either — the land of nod was accessed by a pull-down bed of rock hard proportions. Once in situ the terrible thing filled the entire room, with the tiny Bunsen burner apparatus that justified the apartment being described as 'self-catering' dangerously near the sleepers' heads.

I've stayed in national health hospital corridors that were more comfortable — and at least they are free.

I could however have coped with the spartan gulag-style accommodation if we'd been getting along but after a blissful first day we began to bicker from dawn to dusk. I'm not one of nature's natural stoics and when the hot water system suddenly broke down I sunk into a melancholy from which it was impossible to escape and took refuge in writing poetry. S became moody and irritable: 'I'm going to find a girlfriend I can have some fun with — I can't stand being cooped up with you and your bloody poems!' he scowled.

This set off paroxysms of sobbing and worse poems which made him even crosser as I insisted on reading them out loud to get the syntax right. The broadband connection had also broken down so I was unable to seek solace in Match. com, my usual refuge after one of our rows. We'd hoped to see some of the surrounding scenery but on the first day the exhaust on our hire car had violently exploded, which meant long walks down a steep ravine to the beach and equally long walks up a hill in blistering heat to the nearest supermarket. I was keen to eat out — maybe we would stop quarrelling if we sat in a restaurant — but the nearest was five miles away. And then S took it upon himself to do all the cooking. It was a nightmare and I hold Gordon Ramsay entirely responsible for giving men all over Britain unwarranted amounts of confidence in the culinary arts. I am the queen bee in the kitchen at home and hated being stripped of my authority. There were tearful tussles over the one wooden spoon and the Bunsen burner frequently toppled over as we fought over its control.

Thankfully my spirits lifted after I threw a ceramic yogurt pot at his head, which missed, splattering its messy contents against a wall. The descent into physical violence boosted my spirits and relations began to improve. But it made me wonder, would we ever have a smooth-sailing relationship? We'd have long blissful phases with no arguments and then suddenly, out of nowhere, these fearful spats. But perhaps this is just the way relationships are for some people. Better the passionate ups and desperate downs than the dried up silent indifference I'd endured during my marriage.

However, I've never been so happy to return home and enjoy a blissful reunion with my v-spring mattress, free broadband (unlike most hotels I don't charge myself for this facility), constant hot water and fridge full of exotic food-stuffs hand-picked from Partridges Food Market. Easy access to the Mother Ship (Peter Jones) next door takes care of all my other special needs. How can any holiday destination compete with such *embarras des richesses*?

As philosopher Blaise Pascal put it in 1660: 'I have discovered that all human evil comes from this; man's being unable to sit still in a room.'

How true. If S and I had been content to just sit still in a room at home we would have avoided all those terrible rows. Will we never learn?

Chapter 14

The joys of my wood-burning stove

I'D BEEN talking about greening up my flat with wind turbines, solar panels, rainwater harvesters and converting the
loft using eco-friendly materials for months but, like Gordon
Brown, I'm all talk and no action. Although I'm longing to
crack on — astonishingly, despite living in a conservation
area, I eventually received planning permission for *three*
wind turbines plus everything else we asked for — there is
still the crucial matter of party wall agreements that must be
arranged before work can start.

This means tracking down my neighbours on either side
which is proving tricky. Even trickier, it appears the solicitor
dealing with the matter has disappeared, so we may have to
start the process all over again with a new one. It's ridiculous
that trying to do something positive to reduce one's carbon
footprint should be so expensive and such a bureaucratic
nightmare, although it will become easier in time when
green becomes more mainstream.

Ironically though there are no such obstacles should I
want to book a gas-guzzling flight to Hawaii (I do, very much,
but I'm restraining myself), buy apples from New Zealand or
splash out on shares in planet-wrecking oil companies like

BP and Shell or BAE Systems (makers of landmines and cluster bombs). For those of us who invest in shares, have a bank account or a pension scheme, it's really worth checking out how ethically our funds are invested. Triodos and the Co-op are the greenest banks, but if you want the convenience of the high street, building societies are generally more ethical than ordinary banks.

It proved just as complicated deciding who to employ to do my building work as who I should choose to bank with. Should I plump for Reg, my trustworthy and handsome builder (he looks like a cross between the tall hairy Bee Gee and Jesus, but unfortunately his sex appeal is marred by his squeaky David Beckham voice), or S who is also a good builder? I was wary of employing him, as I worried our volatile relationship might not survive the rigours of building work. Besides, every time I asked him to do something handy it ended in a major breakage of some kind. When he replaced the wasteful halogen bulbs in the kitchen with eco-friendly ones — a horrible job that involves balancing precariously on the kitchen worktop (an interesting marbleised surface created from melted down recycled mobile phones)—he steadied himself by grabbing a cupboard door and ripping it off its hinges. And then there was the time he installed a smoke alarm, which involved climbing onto one of my few remaining Biedermeier chairs, which immediately collapsed. There have been other disasters too.

When handsome Reg with the high-pitched voice came round to do a quote for the building work he kindly offered to take away the Biedermeier chair and mend it, but that was months ago. If I employ S to do the building work Reg will be gutted — it will be even worse than changing hairdressers. More worryingly will I ever get back the chair that was a wedding present and legacy from my Stepford wife incarnation?

Biedermeier has gone through the roof and I can't afford to buy any more of it. Besides, antique furniture is so much more eco-friendly than new stuff.

But whenever I raise this thorny employment issue and voice my doubts S and I end up having a huge row, with him storming off in a terrible huff.

But now, after some thought, I've decided he is the right person for the job. I can't face the prospect of strange builders and he's really behind what I'm doing and intrigued by the possibilities of a green building job. It will be fun working on the project together. Won't it? But nobody shared my enthusiasm. My mother insisted it would end it tears and Donnachadh said I was mad, while Alex's glum silence spoke volumes. I gave their disapproval serious thought then gave S the go-ahead anyway.

When I grumble about the trials of waiting to begin the work, friends say I should be in no great rush to get the builders in, but it's too late because I already have. For although S keeps his own bachelor pad (I use this term loosely, conjuring up as it does an image of chrome appliances, B and O sound systems and sleek Italian furniture, the reality is, ahem, very different), he is already fairly much in situ at my place which, were it not for the assiduous attentions of my various cleaners, would be knee-deep in beer bottles, ravaged tabloids, packets of crisps, grubby cups half full of old tea, fantasy football leaflets and piles of old newspaper coupons of which when you collect ten you get some Bear Grylls Extreme Survival (yawn) DVDs (I know these will never be sent off but I am forbidden from throwing them away). Sometimes my place looks like a building site although no actual building work is actually going on. Heaven knows what it will be like when he is multiplied by ten and work begins properly.

Despite my impatience, work won't be starting for quite

a bit. Salt is rubbed in my impatient wound as I keep seeing pictures of David Cameron's partially dismantled house on the news. Like me he has also employed Alex — a tenuous link with the bastions of power which once gave me a frisson of excitement, but not any more. In the time I've been waiting for planning permission Cameron's house has already been practically knocked down and rebuilt.

I can't help but feel things are going so slowly because, since being taken on by Cameron, Alex has shot into the stratosphere and is now frantically busy tending to the arcane ecotectural needs of his glittering clientele, as well as working with Richard 'moon traveller' Branson to find the solution to global warming with a series of experimental tidal and wind systems on the mysteriously named Energy Island in the Caribbean. It all sounds very promising and rather Dr Moreau.

But it means I can't open a paper or magazine without seeing him and his equally handsome partner (partner in the business sense you understand — each of them has a clutch of glamorous wives and beautiful blonde children who are frequently photographed jumping into one of their eco-friendly self-cleaning ponds) leaning casually against the backdrop of a glossy reclaimed floor, their hands casually in the pockets of their jeans, staring moodily into the camera. They're like a couple of pop stars. Pass the smelling salts!

How on earth can my modest project keep up with this lot and their underground swimming pools, trips to the moon and energy generating islands in the West Indies? I've barely got enough energy to get out of bed in the morning, let alone to power a whole island.

I confessed my status anxiety to Donnachadh when he came round for his bi-annual eco-check-up during which he verifies that I've made the adjustments I swore I'd make during his previous visit. It's a bit like going to the dentist but more guilt inducing. 'Have you tried meditating about it?' he suggested. 'I don't meditate, I chant,' I explained crossly, kicking a box of Perrier water a bit further under the bed. Honestly, sometimes he doesn't listen to a word I say.

With due reflection, of course, it's obvious I'm getting entirely the wrong end of the green stick anyway. I'm buying into the nonsense that being eco-friendly is about purchasing more and doing more when in essence being green is instead about *not* doing than doing. It's about lying around in fields and getting off the treadmill of working 24/7 just so we can buy more stuff we really don't need.

So instead of installing expensive wind turbines and solar panels the emphasis should be on reducing my energy needs in the first place. Of course, sourcing our power from natural means is the way to go but I need to go back to basics — turn down my thermostat, wear extra clothes when it's chilly and boost myself with the thought that the body burns more calories when it's cold. Besides, it's become increasingly clear that domestic wind turbines in big cities provide minimal energy, so for the moment your money is better spent elsewhere. Donnachadh's turbine only provides about £1.60 worth of electricity a year, but he doesn't regret it, as it has generated great interest and helped to demystify wind power. Visitors to his house are riveted by it, so for the moment the turbine earns its keep as an attractive wind 'sculpture' and subject of discussion for passers-by. Besides, with more research and time there is a good chance they may become viable in the future.

Other vital improvements include insulation, installing a water meter (a great way of reducing water usage, as you pay as you use and thus have an incentive to use less), switching off lights and transferring to an energy supplier that sources its energy from renewable sources. It's not as groovy as a turbine whizzing around on my roof but it's more effective.

One of the most energy and money saving things I've done is to install a wood-burning stove (well, I didn't personally — I got S to do it). This means we have now joined the growing band of 'woodies' who power their homes with pellets which are a waste product from the forestry industry. We don't even need to buy pellets, as the mania for home renovation means there is stacks of waste wood lying around in skips for the taking — if not liberated this will end up in landfill where it will take years to rot, creating methane and contributing to global warming.

But what about smoke pollution, I hear you cry, as visions of peasoupy 1950s-style fog cloud your brain. Well we're not talking open fires here; modern stoves are so high tech they are clean enough to be legally used in urban smoke-free zones. But do be careful to liberate only untreated wood and avoid MDF like the plague, as burning it creates a toxic stink. Even so there is plenty of good stuff to go round.

It's a mystery why there is so little awareness of the benefits of using wood as a fuel in this country. We're familiar with wind, tidal and solar renewables, but for many of us wood is a very accessible form of energy. Many areas of the country are richly forested, especially Sussex and the North East, and wood can be easily harvested and coppiced from annual crop growth. Wood heat does not 'deforest' the region; it is borne out of a controlled forestry programme and will actually stimulate more tree planting activity. It is also carbon neutral, as the carbon released through the burning of wood fuel is equal to the carbon the tree absorbed during growth.

A hidden benefit is that a wood-burning stove will

rejuvenate the man in your life. Collecting wood will reawaken his Neanderthal hunter-gatherer impulses sadly deactivated by modern living and make him feel useful again. Instead of staggering in from the pub empty handed, he will arrive wreathed in smiles and bearing fuel. To a woman, a fire is a fire — attractive, warm and cosy. Period. But to men, fires are primal, exciting and a direct link to their caveman pasts, where needs and lusts were quickly satisfied; a world where mortgage repayments, feminism, male grooming and stressful commutes did not exist. S is very emotional about 'his' fire and likes to sit watching it for hours. It has to be made in a certain way and he gets very cross when I interfere. (I swear I don't want to — making fires is a grubby business even if you wear surgical gloves. The few times I have tried I've purposefully done such a rotten job I've been forbidden from going near it.)

The only drawback to our wood-burning stove was that the company simply delivered it without installing it. As I live on the top floor with no lift, this meant long-suffering S had to lug it up the stairs and fit it himself — something that made me faint with gratitude, as it saved a considerable fee. The fact that he now has to see an osteopath every few weeks is an added hidden expense I must confess. But a warm fire is just the thing for a bad back.

It's also extremely economical. My heating bill is now practically zero, as I've been able to turn off all my radiators, thus within a year my £500 stove will have paid for itself.

Rewind! When I showed this bit to Donnachadh he pointed out that this is a fearful lie. 'You can't say your stove is carbon neutral if all your radiators are still on!' he scolded, making me feel a bit guilty. I was going for a quick green hit when the reality is actually a bit more complicated (isn't it always?).

The truth is my bills would be very low if I was able to turn off my radiators. But I can't do this because they are attached to the communal heating system and half of them are mysteriously jammed on all the time. My saintly neighbour Chuck runs the house and controls the boiler but the trouble is that he is from Arizona and favours tropical temperatures. I've begged him to turn down the heating to a more British string-saving temperature, but being American he hasn't really come to grips with the concept of global warming at all. I've tried lobbying my friend Summer, his gorgeous Naomi Campbell look-alike inamorata, but she likes to be toasty too.

Apparently before I can turn off the radiators the system must be 'drained', which means all heating and water must be turned off for the entire house for a day. Not only that but our knee-tremblingly handsome plumber, Bob — the only man in the world who understands the arcane nuances of the house plumbing and can do this terrible draining — has just come back from his sumptuous holiday home in Tenerife and decided to become a fireman. I anticipate fires being lit by ladies all over Chelsea ... perhaps I should just burn our house down and start again. It would be a lot easier.

But back to handsome Bob — he really is quite extraordinary. He once mended an airlock in the heating system by sucking one of my taps so hard that the water whooshed up from the basement and hey presto my water was running again. I nearly fainted with admiration. Really he will be wasted as a fireman.

And as for Donnachadh, I wish he wouldn't always be so damn literal. I'm doing my best under the most TRYING CIRCUMSTANCES!

In gratitude for installing the stove (Donnachadh paid £2,000 to have his installed, but unlike me he wasn't sleeping with his builder), I treated S and I to a swish mini-break in Hastings, known ever after as the Battle of Hastings, as it was the scene of a furious row.

In the early days it was quite tricky sorting out remuneration between us for this sort of thing. I couldn't reasonably expect him to spend all his free time doing DIY for me for nothing (unfortunately) as he doesn't even live here, but as time goes on we've sorted out a satisfactory quid pro quo in which we barter building work with travel. It works pretty well. Most of the time.

I mentioned earlier that when we first starting going out together the difference in our financial situations and backgrounds did make things very awkward. Society still expects men to be the breadwinner and few people, including us, thought we'd survive as a couple for more than a few months. Although the last thing I wanted was some poncy high-spending Porsche-driving banker for a boyfriend (rich but can't mend a fuse) I've always splashed out when it comes to travel.

It's feeble to admit, but I couldn't see much of a future with a boyfriend whose idea of a good holiday was a 4 a.m. Ryanair flight to somewhere I'd pay not to go — it just seemed to symbolise all the differences between us. His happy-go-lucky nature was at first so attractive and his easy going lack of ambition had complemented my hyper-driven nature. Given half the chance he'd be lying around in fields most of the time — the only thing stopping him was that we live in central London and there aren't any. By now I had learnt that it was OK to slow down and just collapse in front of the TV sometimes without feeling guilty. But coming from an overachieving family this was sometimes hard and I found myself longing to make him more driven, more successful.

At that time he was increasingly fed up with being a

builder and had fallen in love with acting. To that end he'd joined a stage company that put on plays several times a year. He was good and was crazy about it but I couldn't understand why he didn't go for it, get an agent, a website and go to auditions and whatever else you have to do to make it as an actor. I made suggestions but these only made him terribly irritated and cross. So, after many frustrating quarrels I gave up trying to push him to do things, and we were much happier for it. Truthfully, I had my hands full with my own ambitions anyway and it was a great relief to have just them to focus on. It's a cliché but you really can't change people, you can only change yourself.

By stepping back and being more accepting I realised that we were hugely compatible as we were. To be with someone as driven as me would be a nightmare. S had the confidence, stability and generosity to relish any success I had and he was very supportive — far more supportive than any other man I'd been involved with.

But this enlightened view was some time coming and arguments were frequent and furious. We'd have a row, I'd throw his clothes out of the window and he would cycle off, not calling for a few days, which made me sick with misery. We were a bit like Elizabeth Taylor and Richard Burton but without the cleavage or the diamonds.

Fortunately, when I began to focus on the good things about our relationship the problems began to shrink. Quite naturally we slowly reached a modus vivendi. But it's a knotty subject and one which still inspires passionate articles in the women's pages of the newspapers. The *Daily Mail* once spent a whole week discussing the pros and cons of alpha vs. beta males. I couldn't resist joining in. My article, excitably headlined 'The socialite and the builder' (though how I could possibly be described as a socialite when I never went out was a mystery), was illustrated with an unflattering picture of me (S admirably refused point blank to be photographed) revealing my roots in their untouched-up glory. This inspired cruel opprobrium on the message boards. 'If she has all this money', grumbled one disgruntled reader, 'you'd think she could spend some of it getting her roots done.' Touché!

Anyway, during the Battle of Hastings — my grateful reward for the horrors inflicted on his back for installing the stove — things came to a head. Again.

It all started so promisingly. I was having a spiritual shopping relapse so we dropped in on an astrologer of high repute on the way who told us how compatible we were. Hurrah! (I'd temporarily forgotten that I'd consulted an astrologer many years ago before I'd got married, who'd similarly assured me that my ex-husband and I were a match made in heaven. That will be £100 please. Ching!)

Feeling chipper, we checked in to a sumptuous all-white hotel overlooking the pebbly beach in Hastings. We had a lovely bright room, replete with a trendy free-standing bath in the middle of the bathroom and an enormous telescope with which to look out to sea. The bed was quite small and hard (how I wish they'd spent less on the groovy telescope and more on the bed) and S had quite a bit to drink during dinner which made him twitch all night. OK, I am very princess and the pea about sleeping — I need complete silence, a sleep mask, a battery of natural and unnatural sleep aids and acres of space — so the twitching drove me to distraction.

'Stop it!' I kept shouting, prodding him with fists and shoes as he lurched from side to side. We had a sleepless night and were both so fed up in the morning we didn't speak and had a terrible quarrel on the stony beach walking to the station.

'Well, perhaps we should call it a day then,' I grumped.

'Yes, I think so, it's just not working out,' he grunted, stomping through the shingles. 'But you don't mean that!' I cried into the blustery gale as he marched angrily ahead. He was white with rage and I really thought this was it. The thought of losing him was too much to bear — my stomach twisted in agony and tears ran down my face. We didn't speak until we got onto the train where thank heavens we made up somewhere between Bexhill and Cooden Beach. Incidentally, I spent my formative years at an obscure boarding school in Bexhill, so perhaps this was symbolic in some way.

Helen Mirren, interviewed during the filming of *The Last Station,* a film about the volatile relationship between Tolstoy and his wife, sums up the ups and downs of love beautifully: 'Love goes through so many phases. When you fall in love with someone, you have no idea where it's going to end up, or the kind of challenges you're going to have to face with each other. Very often, it doesn't last.'

She added: 'There's a wonderful line, which I just love, where Tolstoy says to Sophie, his wife, "Why do you make it so difficult?" and she replies: "Why should it be easy? I'm the work of your life and you are the work of mine," and that's what love is.'

Despite taking this philosophical view of our furious arguments, the stress of them still triggered off agonising bouts of cystitis which I eventually knocked on the head with an amazing supplement called Waterfall D-Mannose, which prevents bacteria from adhering to the lining of the bladder (this may seem like too much information but, trust me, if you are a sufferer you will be happy to try anything).

Increasingly, travel is less of a flashpoint issue anyway. It takes so much effort to go anywhere. Sometimes I'm so overwhelmed with choice and the complexity of booking a trip, I give up and stay at home. It's so much more relaxing.

Chapter 15

Green celebrity hubris

AT ONE time, being green was seen as the dreary province of impoverished, bearded bean-munchers, whereas now it's almost the opposite and there's a danger that living the green life is seen as the province of the rich — an expensive add-on rather than a less glamorous but essential reduction of what we consume. After all, buying organic food, employing swoony ecotects and shelling out for organic cotton clothes are all pricey pursuits.

It's actually very hard to be green and wealthy. The less money you have, the less you buy, the less you travel and you're less likely to run a car. Despite the growth of low-cost flights and cheap imported food there is no getting around the fact that the average wealthy Westerner has a massive carbon footprint while the world's poorest have the least. Even Westerners on low incomes who annually produce about three tonnes per person are emitting the equivalent of about thirty Bangladeshis.

Tom Hodgkinson, editor of *The Idler*, reckons that the habits of the wealthy and their addiction to relentless doing (buying, consuming, travelling) is the prime cause of the world's problems.

'One way to avoid environmental catastrophe', he writes, 'would be not to end poverty but to end wealth. It is wealth, not poverty that makes the problems ... This is why I would recommend that every family and individual try to earn and spend less money, not more. Use your imagination to live well on less each year. This way you will consume less and so create less pressure on the world's resources. Ending global wealth may be the only way out of our predicaments.'

Indeed, if you're worth a few bob you're more likely to own several houses, cars, enjoy scores of extravagant holidays a year and travel extensively (in business class, which uses up more space and thus more carbon per person).

If you have the funds you may even be tempted to take a leaf out of John Travolta's book and buy a few Learjets and turn your garden into a mini-airport — one step further than paving over the front garden so you can park your car. I can't resist sharing a particularly amusing burst of green celebrity hubris. Mr Travolta, a passionate pilot and owner of a £2 million Boeing 707, three Gulfstream jets and a Learjet, plus his own private runway, has encouraged his fans to 'do their bit' to tackle global warming on his website. Clocking up at least 30,000 flying miles in 2007 means he has produced an estimated eight hundred tons of carbon emissions — nearly one hundred times the average Briton's tally. A classic case of do as I say not as I do!

Other *soi-disant* eco-minded celebs are photographed sipping organic smoothies, extolling the virtues of the Toyota Prius and the importance of switching appliances off at the mains, yet seem oblivious to the fact that their penchant for first-class air travel, alligator skin handbags and shoes (they skin the alligators alive!) and carbon-busting lifestyles undo all their greenie points. In mitigation it is very hard once you've got used to a certain lifestyle to give aspects of it up.

But I get exasperated when I see articles about 'green celebrities'. Green celebrity is an oxymoron — the two just don't go together (with the exception of wonderful Daryl Hannah who really is doing it for real).

The truth is that the very things that fuel celebrity are the things that are destroying the planet. We live in a world where talentless, publicity-seeking wannabes are feted for their mindlessness and real heroes go unrewarded. Soap stars and WAGS parade their endless new clothes and accessories manufactured from fur, leather, reptile, even pony. (There is an assumption that pony skin is cow leather but it's not — pony is pony, as in small horse! Besides, what's the difference between a cute horse and a cute cow anyway?)

Meanwhile, each new celebrity outfit provides fodder for the many gossip and fashion mags that have sprung up in recent years. Celebrities and the media that feeds off them endorse the belief that beauty, wealth, private jets, swanky houses and the endless, pointless acquisition of stuff will make us happy. And so they promote and reflect a culture which revels in the short-term acquisition of shoddily produced goods, manufactured cheaply in terrible conditions by third-world outreach workers paid a pittance — possessions which will be discarded as soon as the next must-have product is promoted as the next big thing.

Bobby Kennedy lambasted the media during his stunning speech at the Live Earth concert in 2007 (the best thing during the whole day by a long chalk and worth checking out on YouTube): 'We have a press that has completely let down democracy. That's giving us Anna Nicole Smith and Paris Hilton instead of the issues that we need to understand to make rational decisions in a democracy — like global warming.'

I too wonder why we are constantly fed this pap about

the non-doings of actors and soap stars when the world is full of extraordinary people doing extraordinary things. If only we had the beautiful and brave Wangari Maathai, the Kenyan doctor who set up Kenya's Green Belt Movement, or Muhammad Yunus, 'banker to the poor', Nobel Laureate economist and founder of the Grameen Bank in Bangladesh, who has lifted 1.5 million people out of poverty — instead of actors and celebrities who lambast the intrusiveness of the media on one hand while feeding their interest by posing for magazines and giving endless interviews with the other. Why do we read so much about these people when they have nothing very interesting, original or helpful to say? Lady Antonia Fraser appraised Victoria Beckham as the world's most overrated personage: 'I can't bear all the endless photos of that unsmiling face. I rather think it should be regarded as private grief.'

Celebrities. Bah humbug.

Anyway, there's no point fretting about John Travolta and his Learjets — I can't do much about that. What I *can* do is change my own life and mini-fiefdom, and, as Gandhi put it so beautifully, to be the change I want to see. But although I may be living the change I want to see, I often wonder if very many others really are.

It is dispiriting to discover that while opinion polls suggest that most people in Britain claim to be worried about climate change, there is still little sign of action on their part. One of the main reasons for this may be that they feel it won't make a difference to the bigger global picture. With China, for example, overtaking the US as the world's biggest emitter of carbon dioxide, what's the point of one person using energy-efficient light bulbs or half filling their kettle?

Good point. But more optimistic greens insist these

seemingly small individual steps are a vital tool in averting climate chaos. And as the philosopher Edmund Burke wrote: 'Nobody made a greater mistake than he who did nothing because he could do only a little.' Until recently my focus was on taking personal action on the domestic front but some environmentalists think we should change the emphasis. Robert Kennedy Jr put it thus at the Live Earth jamboree, which as you can see made quite an impression (the fact that he is preternaturally handsome has nothing to do with it).

'Now you've heard today', he yelled above the crowd, 'a lot of people say that there are many little things that you all can do to avert climate change on your own. But I will tell you this, more important than buying compact fluorescent light bulbs or buying a fuel efficient automobile, the most important thing you can do is to get involved in the political process and get rid of all of these rotten politicians that we have in Washington DC.'

While I think it is crucial that individuals change their light bulbs and reduce their personal carbon emissions, not enough of us are making any changes. Emissions continue to escalate due to public apathy and our politicians insist something must be done but do nothing.

For change to happen we need to be politically engaged and vote for politicians who have the guts and courage to avert the worst of global warming with tough, possibly unpopular measures. Currently we are cursed with politicians in the UK, who while not being as obviously corrupt as those Robert Kennedy Jr mentions in Washington, are still enthralled by big business and who measure success in economic growth, airport expansion, road building and the limitless acquiring of new stuff — the very things that are contributing to global meltdown.

Thank goodness for the growth of NVDA (non-violent

direct action) and groups like Plane Stupid and Camp for Climate Action who use wit and ingenuity to raise awareness of the issues politicians won't engage with. Instead of watching in despair as environmental issues are sidelined and airports and roads expand, joining groups like these can give us a voice that our so called 'democracy' does not. If enough people show with their lives and behaviour they are ready to change, politicians will think there are votes in this, and legislate accordingly. The *Daily Mail's* populist campaign to ban plastic bags in 2008 made the lily-livered Gordon Brown finally agree to put a charge on them; he didn't have the courage to do this until he saw voters were really behind such a measure.

Twenty years ago who'd have thought we'd put up with an interventionist nanny government which has banned hunting, smoking in public places, and which uses its authority to further shrink our freedoms by attempting to ban anything from bouncy castles and bunting to St George's Day Parades and conker fights.

Meanwhile, London fire crews have been forbidden from making home visits to offer safety advice to people who smoke unless the residents stub out all cigarettes at least one hour beforehand — all in the name of 'health and safety'. Yet ironically, when it comes to rational and much-needed legislation to guarantee the future of our species the government opts out entirely.

Therefore it is important that those of us who wish to avert global crisis join forces to act collectively as well as individually. For, keen to ensure their own survival, if not the planet's, once politicians realise people want action they may start to pass laws that will make this happen.

It is vital, as Kennedy says, to elect politicians who have the courage to do the right thing by all of us. How disappointing then, that so many green-minded potential voters can't be arsed to vote. I talked to three after the 2008 London elections in which I stood as an assembly candidate for the Greens (I didn't win by the way): the young man who runs a local organic vegetable stall at the farmers market confessed he 'couldn't be bothered', a reflexologist had 'forgotten' to register and a bright graduate who worked in the local health shop 'just didn't get round to it'. All three of them said they would have voted for the Green Party. What a waste! One of Boris Johnson's first actions when becoming mayor was to scrap the proposed congestion charge on heavily polluting SUVs coming into London, just one of the newly elected Tory's policies that made these putative Greens tear their hair in frustration.

While we cross our fingers and hope our politicians will lead from the front it is still worth doing our bit. As Gandhi said, 'Almost everything you do will seem insignificant, but it is important that you do it.'

And, as Bobby Kennedy's equally eloquent father said in a 1968 speech that was actually about apartheid but can be applied just as well to any issue that requires us to stand up and be counted: 'Each time a man stands up for an idea, or acts to improve the lot of others, or strikes out against injustice, he sends forth a tiny ripple of hope, and crossing each other from a million different centres of energy and daring, those ripples build a current that can sweep down the mightiest walls of oppression and resistance.'

Chapter 16

Fortune favours the bold

WITH green issues at the top of the news agenda I'd been longing to present a green TV programme for months. Virgil wrote 'fortune favours the bold', and following this guidance I'd been very proactive, constantly sending in programme ideas, following up leads and ringing people up. Every Telly Tristan in media-land must be aware by now of my great green programme format. Surely.

Although Radio 4 has done a great job of weaving eco-issues into its general format, television has yet to do the same. I had endless meetings with TV execs which never seemed to materialise into anything concrete. I'd got terrifically excited when one respected independent television producer, who as luck would have it actually was called Tristan, took a shine to one of my green ideas and touted it around all the TV stations.

We thought we'd have more luck if I employed a PR agent to get me a bit better known and more TV friendly. Tristan had just started dating an attractive lady who was then famous for successfully remodelling herself from plain Jane to head-turning blonde bombshell, via an exhaustive regime of plastic surgery operations. She was great friends with PR maven, Tilly Brewster, doyenne of café society — she regularly appeared in the dubious television series *From Ladette to Lady* in which a group of working class girls were transformed into Sloane Rangers — who Tristan thought might be just the woman to get me some puff. I wasn't at all sure about this, but knowing he was keen and sensing it would bring him Brownie points with his new girlfriend, I offered to take them all out to lunch and suggested a number of good places I knew.

'Oh no,' he replied, shocked. 'I don't think we could expect ladies like Tilly Brewster and Bonnie to lunch anywhere but the Cipriani or the Ivy ... or somewhere like that.'

You'd think Princess Diana and Jackie Kennedy had risen from the dead in time for lunch the way he was carrying on, but, whatever! Anyway, I ended up treating them to a slap-up lunch at the fancy shmancy Cipriani restaurant, favourite of Russian oligarchs and the glamorati in Mayfair. It was an exhausting charade. In the cold light of day Bonnie looked strangely lopsided and as Tilly rattled on, occasionally breaking off to wave at the various trout-pouted, lizard-skinned *femmes d'uncertain âge* on neighbouring tables, I shuddered and wondered what on earth I was doing there. It reminded me of my canapé-sodden past and I offered up a prayer of gratitude that I no longer had to live that sort of rubbish life any more.

Tristan was very disappointed that I didn't employ Tilly Brewster to do my PR (I wondered if Bonnie was getting some sort of introduction fee, he seemed so disappointed) and his interest in things green deflated like a balloon immediately afterwards. But I couldn't give up my TV aspirations and kept persevering.

Soon after, Donnachadh and I met for lunch at the

scrumptious vegetarian restaurant Govindas in Soho. It was one tenth of the price of the Cipriani but so much more delicious and relaxed. We sat munching scrumptious falafels on the sun-drenched grass in Soho Square and grumbled about endless meetings with Telly Tristans that never seemed to lead anywhere. He'd similarly been plugging away but with no luck.

'Why do we keep hitting so many brick walls?' I wondered. 'Maybe I want to do television too much? S says they can smell my desperation and it puts them off.'

'It's tough,' added Donnachadh. 'It's a fine line between wanting something and wanting it too much.'

It's all a mystery. My life coach had always promoted taking action until one got results. But could one take too much action? I know Virgil insisted that fortune favours the bold, but being bold didn't work for Amelia Earhart, did it? She was so bold she ended up disappearing into the Pacific never to be seen again.

While I was busy bothering telly execs, S was far more gainfully employed painting my flat with eco-friendly paint. I was hugely grateful for his handiness around the house, and it made my married girlfriends hugely envious. While they were fond of their stiff-upper-lip public school husbands, time and propinquity had been the enemy of any sexual frisson and many relationships had deflated to that of brother and sister. I mean, who wants to sleep with a sibling — it's not natural, is it? They often found themselves secretly fantasising about their practical super-handy Neanderthal builders, who were employed at considerable expense to fit their swanky new kitchens. It seemed I was having my cake and eating it for once. With men becoming increasingly politically correct and metrosexual, there is a real gap in the market for the football supporting, beer drinking, handy and slightly unwashed male who is a stranger to male grooming products and gyms, but I don't think men realise this.

S and I had gone to considerable trouble to seek out the most eco-friendly paints we could find. There is a vague but general belief that most of the fancy ranges of paints — Farrow and Ball and the like — must be OK as they are so expensive, but no. They are better than the standard ranges like Dulux, Leyland and so on, but if you want the purest paints available best to go for a dedicated eco-friendly range.

However, all paints are definitely better than they were. Many are now water based and have lower VOCs (volatile organic compounds that create ozone and are implicated in asthma and many health problems) than ever before.

However, they still contain toxic ingredients like cadmium and turpentine and are pointlessly tested on animals. So as I'm trying to lead from the front they don't cut the mustard. These days we're spoilt for choice, as there are an increasing number of excellent natural paint ranges but I settled on Ecos Paints because it had a clear website offering a good range of colours and a speedy delivery service.

It was a huge relief to replace the startling 'fire engine red' walls with calming light Swedish tones. It was painted scarlet many years ago when I was going through an intense feng shui phase and had become a slave to the advice of most of London's top feng shui consultants and even ended up dating one of them, which saved me a fortune — these guys will charge £200 just to come and tweak your crystals but Gaia kept mine spinning for free.

These days we've all moved on from feng shui — like Smallbone kitchens and Stavros's 'Loads-a-Money' it was an eighties fashion that has departed to the great shoulder pad in the sky. But in the noughties it was still quite usual for people (well me) to endlessly shuffle furniture around, paint walls hideous colours and even move house on the spurious advice of their feng shui expert and his omniscient dousing rod.

All my feng shui men said wildly different things. One said I must paint the entire flat blue, as it needed to be 'drained' (I have no idea what from) but Gaia (his real name was Wayne but like many of the esoterically inclined he had changed it to something less earthbound) insisted it must be red. And, indeed, living in a crimson apartment is very energy boosting — if you go for the stimulating brothel look. But quite suddenly it was just too much.

I still believe the colour and arrangement of your living space can influence your mood and well-being but these days I just go for what I like. A contented balanced person will create the right sort of living space for them; therefore a transformation of the person is the key. This is Buddhist philosophy and is really just sound common sense. However, common sense is not always readily available for those of us of the spiritual shopping tendency.

Progress on the painting front was slower than it might be due to a sudden and unseasonable burst of hot weather which meant I keep dragging S off to the Serpentine Lido in Hyde Park for energising swims.

During hot spells this Elysian paradise is crammed chock-a-bloc with permatanned lounge lizardy types all chatting each other up energetically. If you are a glam over 60 and looking for a hot date on a Saturday night — in fact any night at all, even perhaps a daytime assignation — it's the place to be.

Swimming *au naturel* amongst swans and ducks makes the city feel miles away and leaves one feeling a million dollars.

The Serpentine water is fed by its own artesian spring and is so clean it has Blue Flag status. Occasionally there is a bit of a drama when the lifeguard stomps around shouting 'Algae alert!' (Don't panic Mr Mainwaring!), which puts off the feeble minded but fortunately leaves more room for the rest of us. There's actually nothing wrong with a spot of algae, but due to the dreaded 'elf and safety brigade, unless people are warned about it they can sue if they slip, or some such nonsense.

When it's hot there is sometimes quite a bit of algae about. This causes the exceedingly well groomed metrosexuals (preeny 'new men' who buy male grooming products, wax off all their body hair and must be the only people reading endless 'beauty' articles about spas and pointless himbo beautification rituals) to look at me with anxiety as I emerge, green and dripping with five different types of pond weed, from the water. The trouble is, it gets right into your bikini bottoms and trails out of your crotch like some sort of terrible green discharge. Less Green Goddess, more Green Thrush Monster.

One of the metrosexuals was so concerned he stared at my groin with dismay and asked if I was OK and if it was really safe to swim.

'No, I'm feeling WRETCHED,' I lied, causing him to retreat to his sun lounger with relief.

The thing is, serious swimmers like *moi* need all the space we can get and these metro-men are so well moisturized they leave oil slicks of expensive unguents on the water — far more noxious than any algae. Not only that but their lane discipline leaves much to be desired. I can't understand the fuss about algae — chlorine is far more toxic to us and our environment and yet that is flung with casual abandon into most swimming pools in the land. And it really does make your hair turn green, and unlike the algae, it doesn't wash out. Interestingly, up the road, Harrods charges £150 for an algae wrap but at the Serpentine, I get its beauteous benefits included in the £3.50 entrance fee.

The UK has hundreds of similarly stunning outdoor pools. The excellent organisation, the River and Lake Swimming Association, lists many of them and enthusiastically promotes all open swimming from tidal pools to the sea. But maddeningly these lovely swimming spots, used safely for generations, are under constant threat from the Royal Society for the Prevention of Accidents, as well as the dreaded health and safety lobby, who toil energetically to close them. The latter did their best to close the Hampstead Heath Pond to swimmers on winter mornings but in 2006 a hardy band of local swimmers took them to court where they won a landmark ruling in their favour and managed to see the busybodies off. When delivering his verdict the judge spoke out in favour of 'individual freedom' and against the imposition of a 'grey and dull safety regime'. Hurrah!

The no-nonsense cockney couple who run the Serpentine insist the water is pure enough to drink and as I've gulped enough of it during my swims and felt bouncy and energetic afterwards they may well be right. Not many lakes are fed by their own natural spring, so it's probably much purer than the dodgy overpriced stuff, shipped from round the world and of dubious quality, that we pay a fortune for in supermarkets and restaurants.

The irony of our modern predilection for bottled water hit home during my Tony Robbins jamboree in Fiji where, as I've mentioned, we were proffered the same bottles of Fiji water you see in supermarkets. Extolled by nutritionists and celebrities as the *non plus ultra* of liquids, Fiji Water is apparently rich in silica and is cleverly marketed as a veritable elixir of youth and health. That it now has a worldwide turnover of £20 million is an indication of just how gullible we all are. And that's not all. According to its website, 'Fiji Water never meets the compromised air of the 21st century'.

What a load of old cobblers.

The cruel irony is that while designer grocers in the affluent West are full of Fiji Water, Fijians themselves have limited access to potable drinking water. Unfortunately, corporations have jumped on the bandwagon with alacrity. An ex-chairman of the board of the Perrier corporation once said: 'Typically, 90 percent or more of the cost paid by bottled water consumers goes to things other than the water itself — bottling, packaging, shipping, marketing, retailing, other expenses, and profit. It struck me ... that all you had to do is take the water out of the ground and then sell it for more than the price of wine, milk, or, for that matter, oil.'

Hmm.

While mineral water is promoted as health giving it is actually subject to less rigorous testing and purity standards than those that apply to London's tap water. In addition, there are growing fears that plastic bottles may leach carcinogenic residues into the water. Plastics are basically inert but certain plastics have the ability to release chemicals which may affect human health, wildlife and the environment. One major concern is the possible leaching of hormone-like compounds known as xenoestrogens from plastic bottles into the water they carry. Xenoestrogens act like free radicals and are thought to cause damage to the body tissues, including the liver where they may have an adverse effect on important detoxification enzymes. Another concern is that in the body tissues of both males and females 'over-feminisation' is occurring due to the hormone-mimicking action of these plastic by-products. Could this be the cause of the alarming rise in moobs?

I reckon the water that comes out of the wonderful water filter unit beneath my sink — or Eau de Sloane as I prefer to call it — is far superior. It's pure, it's cheap and avoids me having to lug crates of water into my flat.

Indeed, I feel so evangelical about my home spring that I contacted Claridge's and invited them to be the sole exclusive purveyor of Eau de Sloane. Not only, I explained, does it taste delicious (*entre nous* it doesn't taste of much at all, but then it's only water for heaven's sake), but it is the world's first zero-carbon zero-waste water. I could avoid food miles if I line up some of the Eastern European tuk-tuk drivers who race around Soho to deliver it (for as long as they can stave off deportation anyway) and packaging will be minimal, as I can just use the hordes of discarded bottles that get dumped in my bike basket (people seem to think bike baskets are community bins — if you have a bike basket you'll know what I mean).

Claridge's said their 'water menu' was quite full at the moment but they'd get back to me soon. But that was months ago — maybe I should pop round with some samples.

Chapter 17

Carmageddon

ONE of my gaping green black holes was that I still owned a car. I very rarely drove it — to do so would mean losing the coveted parking space outside my flat — but it had taken me until now to make the break with twenty years of (until recently) enthusiastic driving and sell it. I'd driven Mazda MX5s for twelve years in red, black, navy and now best of all racing green, and this super-manoeuvrable little soft-top (ridiculed for being a hairdresser's *manqué de choix* but I liked it just the same) was part of my life. It was always a relief to know freedom and escape was the turn of an ignition key away.

But cars are one of the largest contributors of carbon dioxide and other emissions from the combustion of oil, so they play a major role in creating climate change. Giving up your car is a hugely positive step, but not, if like me, you become completely dependent on diesel-belching black cabs instead.

If I'm honest, my desire to sell my car was not purely motivated by a desire to cut my emissions, but by the realisation that owning a car in the city was actually reducing the freedom and independence I so valued and was now a costly nuisance. Running a car in London has now become so complicated and prohibitively expensive I'm surprised anyone bothers keeping one at all.

The bureaucracy is bewildering. Collating the insurance, the road tax, MOT, yearly service and worst of all, my much coveted Kensington and Chelsea permit, took weeks of administration. Getting the permit should be relatively straightforward: I own my flat, I live in it and it is agreed that I may keep a car in its vicinity. Not so simple! In reality it involves assembling a bewildering battery of paperwork including the MOT, driving licence, insurance documents, household deeds, passport and proof that one is on the electoral roll (if you're not on the electoral roll they will accept a Fire Arms Certificate — I mean, who do they think I am, Charlton Heston?). It's a full-time job.

Once assembled, one lugs all this paperwork to something called the Car Parking Shop. Shop? Hardly! This hideous institution should have a sign above it saying 'Abandon Hope All Ye Who Enter Here'. It is manned exclusively by the surly wives and girlfriends of traffic wardens, but lacking their compassion and sense of humour. They sit grimly behind bulletproof glass taking a sullen jobsworth delight in rejecting applications by pointing out ridiculously tiny mistakes in the unfortunate supplicant's paperwork. One of them refused to believe I lived in my flat and would not give me a permit until an inspector had visited me at home. You'd think I was a paedophile trying to adopt a child, not park my car!

There was no time or date for this inspection — it would be random and if I wasn't there my permit would be refused. Consequently I was housebound for two weeks. I did nip out for short breaks to feel daylight on my skin and fortunately the Lord smiled on me and miraculously the inspector pitched up when I was at home. But really!

At this fearsome 'shop' I have seen fights break out, Saudi Arabian despots waving £50 bribes, and hysterical alpha mums sobbing and begging, but they show no pity. The grim reapers of the Car Park Shop take no prisoners. However, these autocrats must be praised for doing their bit to reduce carbon emissions; their vigilance has caused hundreds of drivers like me to eschew their cars completely.

If only more of us would come to the same conclusion. More deaths are caused by cars than by armed conflict — annual global traffic deaths number more than 1.2 million and those due to armed conflict around 310,000. In 2004, terrorist acts killed an estimated 1,907 people around the world, a three-fold increase over the year before. Strangely, the world seems to be mobilising massive resources in a counterproductive and misguided attempt to defeat terrorism, though as a cause of death it seems a mere drop in the bucket in comparison with car accidents.

The day I sold my car was one of the most liberating of my life. It was like being set free from a prison of bureaucratic anxiety and expense. Running a car had cost me £4,000 a year, so I could now indulge myself with black cabs and still be quids in.

Cabs. I can't resist them. Like tempting private chauffeurs they zoom up and down my street eager to save me the trouble and stress of public transport and whiz me to my destination unstressed and dry of armpit.

Unfortunately, they are not a green mode of transport (unless you book a cab company like Green Tomato Taxis whose entire fleet consists of Toyota Prius's yet still compare favourably pricewise with normal taxis). And yet even hybrid cars are not the energy saviour many people think. Hybrids run on a self-charging electric motor alongside a petrol engine, which cuts emissions and fuel consumption. But building any new car, even a saintly hybrid, uses a considerable amount of energy and creates pollution during manufacture. There is also the pollution created by disposing of the old car. A used car, on the other hand, starts with a significant advantage: the first owner has already paid off its carbon debt. Therefore one can argue that hanging on to a well-maintained old banger, especially if it is run on recycled cooking oil, will be better for the environment. Ultimately, though, the most environmentally friendly car is one you don't buy.

Donnachadh wrote most firmly in my eco-audit: 'It will compromise your credibility if you turn up to Green conferences and Green Party events in a taxi.' Well, I knew this — that's why I always got them to drop me off around the corner so no one could see.

The trouble is, black cabs run on diesel, which emits less CO_2 than regular petrol but is more polluting and a contributory factor in asthma and respiratory diseases. An electric black cab is due out in 2009 which will eliminate the need for cabbies to buy expensive and polluting diesel, although generating the electricity to charge the vehicles will still create carbon emissions. However, these electric taxis will be expensive, so the greening up of London's black cabs will be some time coming.

While agonising about my taxi habit I was reassured by this considered response from a scientist who was obviously pretty keen on taxis too:

A privately owned car is stationary for most of its life. Every time its cold engine is started a large quantity of emissions are produced. It has a very large amount of inherent energy that was used to manufacture it and supply the raw materials. A taxi carries a lot of people in a day with the engine hardly being stopped; its engine stays at its operating temperature for most of the day and night. OK, it runs on diesel which has detrimental environment effects, but they are increasingly using gas.

He goes on to explain:

100 people taking a taxi is certainly more environmentally friendly than 100 people owning and using a car providing they travel the same number of miles. Also 100 people using taxis certainly take less space than 100 car owners on the road and the parking space they demand. Less car parking space means less rainwater runoff problems.

Impressive, *non*? Unfortunately, at the moment practically all black cabs run on dirty diesel. Under the mayoral rule of Ken Livingstone there was talk of running cabs on biodiesel made from, amongst other sources, old cooking fat, which would otherwise be poured down the drain or carted away to be incinerated. But sadly under the rule of Boris this ingenious way of using waste has yet to materialise.

Biodiesel can be made from a variety of substances, including used cooking oil that can be bought cheaply from restaurants. Pouring waste cooking oil down the drains is bad for the environment and clogs up sewage systems, so restaurants usually have to pay to have it taken away. So what could be more convenient than biodiesel companies paying them to take it off their hands? We've been so conditioned that fuel must be coal based and it's often forgotten that Rudolf Diesel actually developed the first engine to run on peanut oil, which he demonstrated at the World Exhibition in Paris in 1900.

Diesel was a true visionary who believed that biofuel would be the real future of his engine. He said, 'the diesel engine can be fed with vegetable oils and would help considerably in the development of agriculture in the countries which use it. The use of vegetable oils for engine fuels may seem insignificant today. But such oils may become in the course of time as important as the petroleum and coal tar products of the present time.'

After Diesel's death the petroleum industry was rapidly developing and produced a cheap by-product 'diesel fuel' powering a modified 'diesel engine'. Thus, vegetable oil was forgotten as a renewable source of power. How different it could have been if we weren't so dependent on oil — just think of all the oil wars that could have been avoided. Examples of oil wars include the illegal invasion and occupation of Iraq, the repeated attempts to overthrow President Hugo Chávez in Venezuela, the botched coup attempt in Equatorial Guinea and the struggles between local communities and oil companies in Nigeria, Angola and Latin America. You get the picture.

However, the growing expense of oil is leading to many innovative initiatives around the world. In 2004, the Government of the Philippines directed all of its departments to incorporate one per cent by volume of coconut biodiesel in diesel fuel for use in government vehicles. Not to be outdone, London's Southwark and Richmond councils power their vehicles on waste cooking oil. The revolution has begun!

Vegetable oil is relatively expensive, but used oil from the cooking industry is abundant and can be easily and cheaply converted into a biodiesel fuel that will mix in any quantity with conventional diesel. If you can collect your own oil it works out at about 15p a litre. Otherwise you can buy in your waste oil for about 30p, so you are getting diesel for about 45p. This is a big saving on the forecourt price.

The biodiesel movement took off during the fuel crisis in 2000 when campaigners furtively bought up huge stocks of vegetable oil from Asda in Swansea, at first raising no suspicions. 'We just thought they were doing a lot of frying — healthy eating has not hit Swansea in a big way,' explained the store manager.

Meanly, this entrepreneurial spirit was nipped in the bud when transport officials caught on and dished out heavy fines, as they weren't paying duty on their 'fuel'.

Although biodiesel is taxed less than regular diesel the government still needs to offer further incentives to help it become more popular. Ultimately it is best to avoid the need for any fuel by living close to work and shopping locally. However, for those who need to drive, buying locally produced biodiesel will cut carbon emissions, slow global warming, support local entrepreneurs and reduce reliance on dwindling petrochemical resources.

Unfortunately, the biodiesel we see at petrol pumps is likely to have been produced in countries like Brazil by clearing swathes of rain forest to grow oil palm — this is as environmentally destructive as buying regular petrol. Fortunately, there are a growing number of small British companies — one such is goldenfuels — who produce their own from waste cooking oil and will deliver it to your door. But as the government continues to offer no support to these innovative carbon-saving schemes it is a labour of love for them to survive.

Many people think that green legislation will inhibit growth and result in unemployment; but to the contrary, promoting sustainable initiatives like solar panels, insulation and goods made from recycled materials and biofuel from waste, for example, will create wealth and new jobs.

Thankfully the concept of growing crops for biofuels has been discredited — in these times of growing food shortages land should be used to feed people not cars. But it's vital not to throw the baby out with the bathwater and not discredit biofuels made from sustainable sources. No one is arguing that it will provide all our energy needs but it could at least form part of a portfolio of fuel sources.

Ironically, having no car meant it would be impossible for me to try out cooking oil as a form of fuel, besides I would need a diesel engine — you can use biofuel in a regular engine but you must convert your oil into bioethanol which is a different procedure. And now I had no car my ATTD (Addiction To Taxis Disorder) was escalating. To salve my conscience I concocted a plan to convert taxi drivers to the benefits of biodiesel, but first of all I had to find out how to make it myself and then I'd write a leaflet to help me proselytise. In this way I hoped to create a great groundswell of support amongst London cabbies who would be realistically more intrigued by the money-saving benefits than any possible improvement of air quality — the great by-product of being green is that it usually results in saving you shed loads of money too.

You may think learning how to make your own biofuel

is a fairly obscure subject, but it is one that appeals to a certain type of man who is usually found tinkering in sheds and is very good at fixing things — these sorts of men are the backbone of Britain. If you type 'how to make your own biofuel' into any search engine you will find plenty of courses all over the country. We chose one in Wales, held at the Centre for Alternative Technology in Machynlleth. The thing that immediately struck me when we arrived was the astonishingly high ratio of men to women (forty to three).

There are many shortages in the world today, fuel and food being the most worrying, but the shortage of eligible men is also very problematic. Yet the strange thing is that whenever I venture into the streets there seem to be twice as many men than women and yet many of us know hordes of attractive single women who can't find any men for love or money. Are these crowds of men stalking the streets a mirage? Are they gay? Statistically there are ten per cent more men than women between the ages of 20 and 45. If this is the case why can't women, with their inbuilt nest-building tracker devices, sniff them out? But once, in Wales, I realised that a large proportion of these lost men can regularly be discovered attending DIY biodiesel courses. I made a note to tell my single girlfriends to abandon the hairless, over-groomed metrosexuals haunting London's bars and develop an immediate interest in biodiesel instead.

The Centre for Alternative Technology is an eco-haven set in stunning scenery and is entirely fuelled by wind turbines and solar power. It runs fascinating courses on different environmental subjects every weekend but the accommodation was so threadbare and unappealing (acceptable for Shed Men but not for Virgo fusspots like me) we decamped to a friend's very plush non-turbined house around the corner and popped back for classes and delicious vegetarian meals washed down with copious vats of wonderful gooseberry wine.

We soon learnt that making biodiesel yourself is not that easy. I must confess that I did tune out during the seminars and S seemed less than riveted, but this is what I picked up. First you must thin your waste cooking oil with alcohol so it is the same consistency as petrol — a procedure that requires a basic level of chemistry and involves some dangerous chemicals (you really have to know what you're doing). But after one afternoon in the workshop my fellow students were undaunted.

'If you can plumb in a sink it's a piece of piss,' said Ralph over a glass of gooseberry fizz in the bar. I nodded in agreement but knew in my heart that I was as likely to figure out how to plumb in a sink as I am to fly to the moon, but for Shed Man — or I'm sure a typical taxi driver whose brain has been hugely enlarged by learning the Knowledge — the process would be fairly straightforward.

A simpler option is to convert your diesel engine to run on pure cooking oil which will bypass this complicated oil conversion process. Conversion kits are made by a German company called Elsbett, which will supply and install them for about £1,200. Independent research has shown that rather than decreasing performance, cars that are converted to run on pure vegetable oil have an increased power performance as compared to diesel over most speeds.

If you don't want to attend a course you can also get the gist of how to make your own biodiesel at journeytoforever.org, in an article by Mike Pelly, owner of Olympia Green Fuels, who uses biodiesel fuel to power his two cars. He makes the mixture from used vegetable oil discarded by Chinese restaurants and fast-food joints.

Mike sent one enthusiast a full report on how he makes biodiesel. 'It's a result of my work over the past five years along with contributions from other experimenters,' he said. 'Pass it along to anyone you please.'

'It works!' wrote the enthusiast. 'Amazing! Last night we put the stuff in Midori's old diesel Land Rover and it ran like a dream and smelt like a bunch of roses! Well, French fried roses anyway. Now it runs clean, on waste Big Mac residues we brewed up in a bucket in the kitchen, and we're very tickled!'

Chapter 18

I'm a cyclist — don't hate me

THE delights of brewing up my own fuel would of course remain theoretical (thank goodness) as since being released from the dangers of driving I'd splashed out on a new bike. I'd foolishly bought it impulsively and quickly realised we didn't get on at all. It was the cyclist's equivalent of a Porsche when what I wanted was a Mini; it had twenty speeds and was heavy and cumbersome. I'd chain it up to lampposts and it would frequently and most annoyingly topple over, almost purposely I felt, to irritate me.

Even worse, now we both had bikes S got very keen on the idea of cycle rides at the weekend. He had this idea of riding to Battersea Park, which is a good half mile away, cycling around it and then riding home. It sounded exhausting — who did he think I was, the Ironman?

But he seemed to think it would be romantic and began to tout the alarming idea of cycling to Brighton. Maybe I'm missing something, but there is nothing romantic about bicycling together; we bicker on bikes as much as we did in a car. I am 'too slow', 'too fast' or I make 'too much eye contact with drivers', which he thinks makes them more likely to run me down. His lack of confidence in my ability on two wheels makes me dithery. It's like being watched reversing into a parking space — men love to watch women doing this and intimidate them into doing it badly.

I could sometimes be excused games if I pleaded period pain or something, but deep down I wished I could be this happy-go-lucky Cameron Diaz-type girl who could stick a bikini in a backpack and just cycle off for a weekend. Spontaneity goes out of the window when you are compelled to pack a travel kettle, ear plugs, sleep mask, cystitis prevention remedy and two large tablespoons of barley grass powder (I like this mixed into my organic veg juice in the morning) before you can go away for a night. My idea of being devil-may-care is not to pack my juicer; I try to draw the line somewhere.

One of the alarming things about cycling (I don't want to put anyone off — I'm just being frank, OK) is that it's very bad for the skin. Cyclists are like skiers with their splendidly lithe figures topped with windblown and leathery complexions. On the rare occasions I did venture out on two wheels I took the precaution of making sure I was heavily protected with Dr Hauschka biodynamic sun repellent which gave my face an unbecoming ghostly sheen. The other unappealing thing about being a cyclist is that it's like being pregnant — people always want to tell you what to do. I am constantly being told to buy a helmet, but helmets make cyclists look like they know what they're doing and this would surely make me less safe. Wobbling along slowly and erratically meant drivers gave me an enormous girth — sometimes they didn't dare overtake me at all, fearful that I might swerve into them at any moment. But they barely gave professional looking cyclists whizzing along in sweaty day-glo Lycra and alarming warlike pointy helmets any margin of error at all. No, I reckon I'm far better off without one.

Anyway, after several weeks of pedalling misery I decided to secretly give up cycling. It was a relief to succumb to my ATTD full time while I allowed my beastly bike to languish, occasionally toppling over in a light breeze, outside my flat. Maybe, I hoped generously, someone might nick it and give it a better home.

And then one day I was rushing out of my flat about to hail a cab so conveniently driving past (who needs a chauffeur?) and I noticed my bike had gone. Perhaps it had been gone for days but I hadn't noticed. Hallelujah! There is a God I thought, leaping gleefully into the taxi.

But no sooner had I got used to my no-bike bliss when S, eager to resume our bickering bicycle rides, found a broken bike in a skip which he impressively reconditioned to peak condition and presented with a flourish. This bike is a dream to ride — it only has three gears and it never topples over, however carelessly it is propped up. The moral is: you don't always get what you pay for when it comes to bicycles — cheaper can be better.

Unfortunately, the more people that take to their bikes the more anti-cycle hysteria there is. Why do cyclists receive endless condemnation because they may quite naturally decide to edge safely through the odd red light when it is obvious nothing is coming towards them? In America it is legal to turn right at a red light, if safe to do so. Similarly, if it is safer for a cyclist to get ahead at the lights instead of waiting for them to change along with a long queue of revving SUV drivers and terrifying white van men, not too bothered if they crush said cyclist in their rabid race to overtake, why not?

I also don't understand the outrage at the thought of cyclists sometimes using pavements — would they rather cyclists were killed than risk dangerous, busy and narrow roads? Interestingly, cycling on pavements is legal in Japan and Germany and no fatalities have ever been reported. Obviously I'm not recommending wild, crazed and speedy cycling on pavements, but considered and safe pedalling on wide boulevards has got to be an improvement from risky, narrow and congested roads.

In the final reckoning, cars were responsible for more than 2,946 deaths in the UK in 2007 whereas cyclists around one person every two years. More attention should be focused on kamikaze drivers — many of whom drive around clamped to their mobile phone, drinking and eating, putting on make-up and even reading the newspaper.

But not all motorists can be tarnished with the same brush and neither can all cyclists be blamed for the purported sins of the few. There are bad drivers and good drivers in the same way as there are careless cyclists and good cyclists, but the rabid aggression vented on them seems out of all proportion to their sins. I nearly choked on my cappuccino when the usually mild mannered Nigel Havers vented his apoplexy in the *Daily Mail*: 'I am heartily sick of the lot of them. They have made travelling round London a nightmare, whether by foot or by car. What makes me so angry is not just their scorn for civilised road behaviour, but also their conceited self-righteousness.' *Sacre bleu!*

Maybe these anti-cyclists are suffering from the modern affliction of Minor Irritation Syndrome, which causes sufferers to blow up small irritations into major issues. The strangest things seem to work up sane people into unreasonable amounts of rage these days. 'Bogus' asylum seekers used to inspire the most fear and loathing, but this is now seen as being un-PC and possibly an indication of being a secret supporter of the BNP, so the collective spleen has been redirected towards cyclists and wind turbines instead.

I discovered the suspicion and horror with which wind turbines are held when I was invited to open a fete at the King's School, Canterbury. My stepbrother is chaplain there and had generously exaggerated my fete-opening qualifications to the Powers That Be. Although I have had some tuition — I did spend a year at Lucie Clayton where fete opening, slipping into sports cars elegantly and dinner party seating placements were an essential part of the curriculum. I've had practical experience too, as last year I opened Green Party pal Noel's second-hand shop in the Finchley Road.

However, nothing prepared me for the terror of it. Noel's shop contained gems like Barbara Windsor's old knickers but this affair was much grander. There were no antique pants on sale but they did have dancing unisex Kenyan tribesmen, beautiful old books and hordes of gorgeous sixth form girls stalking the sun-drenched grounds like stroppy gazelles.

When I was handed my ribbon-cutting scissors I was rendered quite mute with terror and didn't manage to say very much at all. Retreating in relief I was soon accosted by a smug parent who began a tirade against David Cameron's wind turbine.

'It's a disgrace!' she screeched behind a pair of enormous Jackie O. sunglasses. 'Notting Hill is going to become a nightmare! These turbines will be a blot on the landscape. Not only that but we live next door to a peculiar eco-architect who lives underground!'

'Oh, you must mean Alex,' I replied brightly, desperately seeking rescue. 'He's my ecotect — his house is really wonderful and as far as I can gather is entirely solar powered.'

This didn't console her at all.

'Well, I think it's MOST PECULIAR!'

People like this object to any windmill that isn't in a Constable painting. Would they feel any more comfortable living next to a stonking great nuclear power station, which is what will happen unless we do consider other forms of energy?

The encounter left me feeling strangely disturbed, for soon I shall become one of the most hated women in Britain. Not only am I developing kamikaze cyclist tendencies but I'm hoping to one day be the proud owner of three wind turbines. Thank goodness I'm not a bogus asylum seeker as well.

Chapter 19

My Vogue *moment*

WITH everything eco being so *au courant*, many magazines are churning out 'green' specials. The format is fairly standard: a glam Hollywood actress is put on the cover wearing a green dress and extolling her commitment to buying organic veg and her Toyota Prius. Her private jet habit and penchant for lizard skin handbags are carefully airbrushed out of the picture along with any other unsightly blemishes.

However, I must admit that I'm not averse to a spot of airbrushing myself and didn't exactly show *Vogue* the door when they asked to photograph me for a green issue they were planning. As an inducement they offered me carte blanche to plug my favourite cause, so I jumped at the chance to give some puff to BUAV (British Union for the Abolition of Vivisection), which does such a great job in drawing attention to the plight of laboratory animals. The irony of the thorny and unfashionable issue of animal testing juxtaposed against furs, leathers and beauty products, most of which had been tested on animals, was irresistible.

Another great bonus was the opportunity to enter the famous '*Vogue* Glamatron' and be groomed by a team of Voguettes. The term 'Glamatron' was coined by ex-Condé

Nast girl and best-selling author Wendy Holden to describe the miraculous process during which ordinary looking people are transformed into groomed, glossy, otherworldly creatures. A Glamatron sounds like some sort of heavenly tardis stuffed with wondrous beauty products and cosmetic surgeons, but refers to the huge tarting up operation that models and mortals are subjected to before the average *Vogue* photo shoot.

On the eagerly awaited day of my shoot a team of bright young things flitted into my flat bearing crates of make-up and bags of couture. I welcomed Tottie, the queen bee and top stylist, Arabella, a junior stylist, Fleur, the make-up girl, plus a hairdresser, a writer poised to record my *bon mots*, a gofer and someone else whose purpose was not immediately apparent to the naked eye. After hours of preening, Tottie, a ditzy blonde dressed in a combustible combination of oranges, pinks and reds, dipped into one of her huge bags and hauled out what appeared to be a large green tent.

'This is Vivien Westwood,' she shrieked, her small bony hands shaking with excitement. This wasn't the look I was aiming for at all — I'd hoped for something a bit more streamlined, edgy even. 'You look sewper!' the Voguettes trilled once I'd put it on. Was I the only one who was unaware that I looked like a pond with a big white head sticking out of it?

Before I had time to change my mind I was zipped in and driven to BUAV's offices in North London where I was to be photographed. Alarmed that her charge was wilting into a sea of mud-coloured taffeta, Tottie kept up a stream of chat. 'Are you single Julia?' she enquired breezily, flicking her streaky blonde hair, 'because I've got this lovely man you'd simply adore.'

'Actually I have got a boyfr ...' but she was off again. 'He's called Lionel and he's mad about shooting. He's got this huge estate in Cheshire and he runs an art gallery, adores the theatre, ballet ...'

I shuddered. Lionel the culture-vulture would be no good for me at all but I did not want to appear ungrateful. Instead I took a slug of my Bach Rescue Remedy and sunk a little deeper into my voluminous frock which appeared to be growing into a sort of horrible sludge-coloured triffid — if it got any bigger it would take up the entire backseat of the car. I tried to change the subject but Tottie wasn't having any of it.

'I'm going to RING HIM RIGHT NOW,' she screeched suddenly, reaching into her enormous Louis Vuitton trunk-handbag for her tiny jewel-encrusted mobile.

'Lionel!' she screamed, 'I've got this gorgeous gel, she's longing to meet you ... You're in Chile? On a chairlift!' 'He's skiing,' she hissed to me. 'How amazingggg. Well, I'll give you her number when you're back and you can give her a ring!' I knew he never would but I was touched she'd gone to the trouble.

Eventually we arrived at the BUAV HQ and to avoid getting the bottom of the dress grubby I was hoisted into the building on a makeshift sedan lifted by the Glamatron team who were, it must be said, surprisingly strong and not remotely impeded by their fashionable wedgie shoes or Arabella's feather fascinator, pinned precariously to the top of her long thin head. 'It's OK,' she explained defensively to the receptionist, who was giving it disapproving looks. 'It's bird-friendly — they don't kill the birds, they wait for the feathers to drop naturally, OK?' This was typical fashionista nonsense but in the interests of harmony was not pursued.

Gazing at my entourage as we tottered in, a BUAV girl whispered, 'I'd guess their budget for this one shoot would cover our entire income for a month.' 'More like a year,' I replied gloomily.

After I'd been preened a bit more a scrawny photographer slid through the door and began to jump around like Zebedee on speed, snapping away. He had the skinniest legs I'd ever seen and as he was known as a bit of a Lothario I wondered how any woman could cope with sleeping with a man whose legs were thinner than her arms. I'd find it horribly disconcerting, wouldn't you?

'Gosh you look a-maze-ing,' the Voguettes chimed happily, 'Smile!' Consequently I am grinning inanely, distracted by the photographer and his strange legs, swamped in a pair of mud-coloured curtains with a picture of a monkey having its head sawn off in the background.

The picture was headed excitably, 'The heiress who gave up the champagne lifestyle to go green!'

As if! I only took up drinking when I became an environmentalist — most greens drink like fishes. If James Lovelock's depressing forecast is correct and we've only got twenty good years left, we all need something to boost the spirits.

The other point I want to make is that 'heiress' sounds terribly glitzy and loaded but if you think about it, if one is an heir, one is waiting for someone to die before one comes into this apparent largesse. The reality is that one can be an heiress and not have a bean. Just thought I'd point that out.

After the article came out I was invited by the charity, Animal Defenders International, to squeeze into a small metal cage with Meg Matthews and songwriter Maria Daines, who had released a hit song called 'Monkey in a Cage' to raise awareness for International Primate Day. Horrifically, monkeys and apes are still used in animal experiments despite the opposition of many doctors, scientists, researchers and two hundred welfare groups worldwide, including the RSPCA and primatologist Dr Jane Goodall. —

Used to Green Party photo calls where no one usually turns up, it came as a shock to be confronted with about twenty snappers, lured by Meg Matthews, who as the ex-wife of supergroup Oasis founder member Noel Gallagher, is a paparazzo-pulling celeb. Good for her for using her celebrity clout for something useful. The cameramen kept asking her to take off her sunglasses, 'No, I bloody won't,' she insisted firmly and the specs remained on.

The snapping went on for ages. We were photographed getting into the cage, climbing out of it, on top of it, outside it, under it and pushing it while smiling, looking sad and angrily banging on the bars. Eventually the clicking stopped and we could climb out and all go home but many animals are not so lucky.

Humans are only locked up for life when they have committed some heinous crime but this doesn't apply to animals. Dolphins cruelly captured from the oceans and transported to tiny oceanariums to perform tricks for stupid spectators, wild birds netted and caged and the thousands of monkeys captured in jungles and locked up in cages have committed no crime yet must suffer a life of agonising, often solitary, confinement.

We don't need to capture wild primates then destroy them in labs. While there are similarities between us and primates there are also key biological differences which make primate research unreliable. This was demonstrated in the TGN1412 experimental drug trial in 2006 which nearly killed six young men at Northwick Park Hospital when they were given a drug which had been 'proved safe' in monkeys.

Testing on animals slows down medical progress because it tells us about other animals, not ourselves. Animals react differently to many substances: aspirin, for example, is safe for people, but can be fatal to cats; penicillin can kill guinea pigs; arsenic is dangerous for humans but not for rats, mice or sheep; insulin is safe for humans yet can produce deformities in mice, rabbits and chickens; thalidomide was tested on animals but cripples humans. Given this misleading data it's no surprise that prescription drugs tested on animals are the fourth leading cause of death in the Western world.

It's not just tree huggers like me who are coming out against animal experiments — many scientists and doctors are opposed to them because they believe that they are plain bad science. Thousands of them have joined Europeans for Medical Progress (EMP), an independent charity which opposes animal experimentation solely because it harms people. These are hard-headed professionals brave enough to stick their head over the parapet and say patients are dying due to reliance on misleading animal testing.

When I met EMP director Dr Kathy Archibald at the House of Commons, where they were holding a debate sponsored by their patron, Tony Benn, she explained that those who speak out risk professional suicide and ostracism from the medical establishment but they feel compelled to fight for the truth.

There is now overwhelming evidence that animal experiments can prove misleading or fatal to humans, that they exhaust precious research funding, waste valuable time, produce ineffective solutions and delay progress toward human cures.

Dr Michael Coleman, Senior Lecturer in Toxicology at Aston University, notes: 'As well as the ethical considerations, scientifically, primates are simply not close enough to us to act as good experimental models and we should be promoting replacement of animal work with human cellular systems.

We must leave behind the intellectual laziness of relying on animal models and invest in human cellular based alternatives for the future.'

Many animal experiments are bewilderingly pointless. A huge number of substances are tested — in 2008 there was an outcry when rabbits were forcibly fed lethal doses of cranberry juice. Why? Each new unnecessary cleaning product that is launched must similarly be tested. At Columbia University lead pipes were surgically embedded into the skulls of monkeys to study the connection between stress and menstrual cycles. Very few women have large weights surgically attached to their skulls, but they do suffer from other types of stress — perhaps the realisation that their taxes are wasted on ridiculous experiments like this.

A. N. Wilson put it succinctly: 'Any development which prolongs the life of some poor, drooling old human being is progress, even if it comes from H. G. Wells's *Island of Dr Moreau*.'

Unfortunately, the focus continues to be on a tiny minority of extremists at the expense of rational debate — in reality the majority of animal rights protesters are compassionate and law abiding. The fight against apartheid and slavery and the suffragette movement all had their share of violent extremism but this does not detract from the essential justice of their arguments.

It is ironic that we can't avoid television programmes about people being operated on, while programmes depicting animal experiments are considered too horrific to stomach. This squeamishness means experiments are performed in gulag-type establishments hidden from the public gaze. If the conditions are really as acceptable as supporters insist, why the secrecy? How I wish these barbaric places could be opened up to a fly-on-the-wall documentary so the so-called animal loving public could really know what goes on in them. Then we could begin a rational debate — preferably not financed by pharmaceutical companies or others with a vested interest in perpetuating this iniquitous system, as is currently the case.

The tragic thing is that while we all bicker and pharmaceutical companies line their pockets, in laboratories all over the world animals are suffering unimaginably agonising deaths when there are already far more effective testing methods available. It makes my blood boil. Gandhi said: 'The greatness of a nation and its moral progress can be judged by the way in which its animals are treated.' Judging by the way we treat animals in the supposedly animal-loving UK this could soon mean taking the Great out of Britain.

Chapter 20

Greenwash in Chelsea

BECAUSE of my column I was occasionally asked to speak at eco-conferences. I used to turn down invitations out of fear and lack of confidence but in the spirit of 'if it doesn't kill you it can only make you stronger', I was now gritting my teeth and saying yes. Besides, there are so few women speaking at these green do's I get a lot more leeway than a man does — people are usually so surprised to see a female on the panel at all they give me a relatively easy ride. It reminds me of Dr Johnson who said, 'a woman's preaching is like a dog walking on his hind legs. It's not done well, but you are surprised to find it done at all.' So I'm quids in for just turning up.

It's a huge relief that S will come along and cheer me on — it's so much easier doing these things with a boyfriend. I feel quite proud of myself for all the years I soldiered on, doing equally frightening things like this by myself. Now I've experienced a supportive partner I don't know how I'd cope without one. It's like flying economy — if it is all you've known it's fine, but once you fly first class ... well, going back to economy is unrelenting misery.

Talking of first class, if you book Al Gore for what he

modestly calls his 'slide show', you must also throw in first-class travel and put him up in a fine hotel. I only mention this because I gave Al Gore's superior travel arrangements some envious thought when I gave a talk in Leicester and was put up in a hideous travelling salesman hotel. I took the liberty of upgrading us to the honeymoon suite for an extra fiver, but a couple would have had to love each other very much to survive their first night of marriage in this grim moth-eaten room, with its thin, stained mattress, view of a four-lane motorway and bunch of dusty plastic carnations in the window.

Honeymoons are quite challenging enough as it is; I barely survived mine and that was in five-star luxury in Barbados. I knew I'd made a mistake and I was utterly miserable. I kept looking at my watch every twenty minutes and wondering why time was passing so slowly. But if I'd been stuck in that grimy room with the plastic bouquet I would have thrown myself out of the window.

But looking on the bright side I must point out that we did have a kettle *and tea-making facilities* in our room. No matter how dreadful an English hotel, it will almost always have a kettle, which is a very great thing — avoiding the need to pay through the nose for a cup of tepid water with a separate tea bag on a saucer.

However, I hope I'm not being ungrateful and going against the spirit of positive thinking DVD *The Secret* when I say that this facility was not necessary, as I'd taken the precaution of bringing my own travel kettle plus a mini-boiler as backup if number one kettle broke. Travel kettles are not very reliable and I'd had them break down on me before — it's a complete disaster if you're abroad in a kettle-free zone. How lovely then, that in Leicester I had access to three of them. I bet even Al Gore doesn't have that many.

To be honest I prefer giving lectures close to home. At Chelsea Town Hall I was scheduled to appear with Donnachadh and the dashing ecotects Alex and Tim for a talk about going green in Chelsea. The first thing Donnachadh did was ask for the dazzling lights in the hall to be switched off. Ironically, we were sitting in a hall flooded with natural light with all the lights on and the radiators blazing, despite it being a warm day. Everyone cheered at this revolutionary idea, but the ridiculous thing is that I often attend eco-conferences and lectures bathed in electric light in broad daylight. On cold days doors are flung open and radiators fire away during summer. Once you start becoming energy aware there is no going back and you're doomed to wince forever at lights left on unnecessarily and constantly risk being called a nag by requesting they are turned off.

After Donnachadh had done his stuff, it was the ecotects' turn to stride onto the podium, causing a collective gasp amongst the ladies in the audience — there can't have been so much excitement in the town hall since Cary Grant was rumoured to have attended the cinema across the road in 1949. As Alex launched into his gripping eco-spiel the elderly lady next to me slumped in her seat — it wasn't clear if she was in a swoon or had died, and to my shame I put off investigation as Alex's PowerPoint presentation had me spellbound. Not all of the ancient attendees were so keen though.

'YOUNG MAN, IF YOU'RE GOING TO WHISPER!' boomed a crusty Boer War survivor, 'USE THE MICROPHONE!'

'He's just saving energy,' quipped the local Tory MP Sir Malcolm Rifkind from the podium.

The audience had been getting very excited about all the eco-improvements outlined in the lectures but spirits were soon crushed when the leader of the council proceeded to pour cold water on practically everything.

'Half-filling your kettle is a great idea,' he began, but ... it was 'unrealistic' to expect people to suddenly switch to low-emission light bulbs and putting up solar panels would upset our beautiful Chelsea landscape. If he was that concerned about destroying the character of the area, I wondered, why had the council allowed scores of hideous mini-Tesco's and countless characterless chain stores to be built. Modern solar panels are barely visible and less of an eyesore than the vast white satellite dishes which are now an accepted part of our skyscape. Mind you, this is the man who had supported the demolition of a perfectly good local school when refurbishment would be cheaper and far less wasteful, as well as the selling off of most of its playing fields to property developers. Flogging school playing fields to profit a few fat cats is a national scandal, and surely partly responsible for the growing obesity of schoolchildren who are increasingly cooped up indoors playing computer games when they should be running around outside.

But, of course, like most politicians, this fellow made vague noises about the importance of climate change and then vociferously opposed any real action that might combat it. A bit like David 'green' Cameron who installs a pointless wind turbine on his house and has his photo taken with a few huskies in the Arctic to register his concern about melting icecaps but voted for the Iraq war, supports motorway expansion and backs Trident (which will increase the escalation of weapons around the world and cost billions which could be spent on really valuable measures to combat global warming). But most politicians simply aren't interested in taking courageous action and the only way things will ever change is if individuals take the initiative, which will hopefully make our lily-livered rulers realise there are votes in green measures.

At the end of the lectures the elderly audience, stirred by the thought of the cold buffet waiting for them next door, made a disorderly stampede towards the exit. As we left the empty hall all the lights were switched back on again to collective groans from Alex, Tim, Donnachadh and me. Disheartened? Not us!

Meanwhile, back on the domestic front, S and I had reached a calmer stage in our relationship and we'd reduced our furious rows from once a month to about once every three months. And now, even when we did have a quarrel, we didn't immediately assume it meant we were splitting up. I've noticed that people who come from chaotic backgrounds often assume a nasty argument is the end while those who come from a secure family background are more likely to take the long view and see that rows are sometimes just part of a healthy relationship and will pass.

Work wise things were also going well, so it came as a horrible shock to receive an email out of the blue from one of my editors at *The Independent* sadly informing me that my column was to be 'discontinued'. This was the last thing I'd thought would happen and I wasn't prepared for it at all. More fool me. I should have known that as a freelance columnist I had no security and lived on permanently shaky ground. That I'd survived three years wasn't bad going; as a species, green columnists have a shorter lifespan than average as things eco don't really get the average pulse racing.

Unsurprisingly this depressing news made me very low. It was even more horrible, as the bad news had come via email, but this is the brutal world of newspapers and you like it or lump it. I spent a couple of days stomping around in a daze of shock and misery. S was very understanding but he got on my nerves for something or other so I threw a box of German language cassettes at him. Experience has taught me it's always worth having a big box of cassettes to hand if you're in a 'must chuck something' mood because they make a satisfying amount of clatter and chaos while creating minimal long-term damage. Since we're on this subject, I should point out that throwing an empty watering can against the wall is also very gratifying — plenty of bang for your buck, so to speak. There is usually a split second where one has time to weigh up the pros and cons of throwing something — you certainly don't want to risk a mobile phone or laptop — so best to have plenty of watering cans and cassettes to hand for when you need to let off steam.

When vile things like this happen it forces one to look at things from a different angle. I realised that I'd never been truly at home at the *Indy* — I was probably too right wing and there had been a distinct *froideur* between my editor (a virtuous mother of four) and me since I'd filed a column promoting tax credits for the childless as a way to curb population growth. Besides, being stuck at the back of the paper meant my column was so well-hidden I could barely find it myself sometimes. Donnachadh had once been asked if he was *The Independent*'s Green Goddess, so I can't have made much of a mark. Still it was great while it lasted.

My mood was greatly boosted by a small-minded but delicious feat of revenge. Every year there is an auction of *Independent* columnists for charity. In my capacity as Green Goddess I was sold off to the highest bidder to eco-audit their home. Sod's Law dictated that whoever bought me usually lived in the far north of England, which involved me forking out for an expensive train fare and one night in a local hotel. I never asked the paper for expenses, but this

year, with a time-consuming and e
to green up the altruistic fellow who
looming — and smarting from my disi
had evaporated. Let them find some oth
pay back the man, I thought crossly. I qu
following and emailed it off to my editor:

> *I was all set to go to Durham and do my duty by*
> *however the demise of my column has precipitated a nu*
> *dramatic changes in my life.*
>
> *My (new!) husband and I have quite impulsively decide*
> *to relocate to Honolulu. We have just bought a comfortable*
> *boat in which to sail there and rented an off-grid solar-powered*
> *beach house in Waimea Bay. With the fantastic experience I've*
> *gained writing The Green Goddess I have managed to secure*
> *a regular slot on the* Honolulu Advertiser *describing our*
> *new life.*
>
> *Under the circumstances, I will not now be able to go to*
> *Durham after all. I am very sorry not to carry out this obliga-*
> *tion but husband and crew are keen to set sail ASAP.*
>
> *Mahalo!*
>
> *Julia*

It sounded so plausible I almost started believing it myself
and was quite excited when my editor rang leaving urgent
messages. I was tempted to call her back — maybe she wanted
me to write about my dazzling new beach-bound life? But I
restrained myself.

My naughty email made me feel very chipper. I reminded
myself that when one door closes another one shuts, I mean
opens, and my Buddhist friends kept telling me that it meant
something better lay round the corner.

In Buddhism there is a principle called 'turning poison

nt to know about
opher Dr Daisaku

...n to fly across
...to realize that
...just the time
...om sour but
...s, when all
...pt to lurk

pensive trek to Durham
had bid for my services
...issal — my goodwill
...er mug to do it or
...ckly penned the

Mr Ellis;
...ber of

...ple of changing poison into
...s we base ourselves on faith, we can over-
...difficulty or hardship. We can give meaning to every
challenge and utilize it to our advantage, transforming it into
benefit. When an imposing barrier looms before us, it is actu-
ally an opportunity to expand our life condition and accumu-
late greater good fortune. No matter what, the important thing
is to advance 'day by day and month after month' as steadily
as flowing water, as powerfully as a mighty river.

And so armed with this boosting knowledge and a copy
of *The Secret*, I took myself off to Grayshott health farm for a
few days. *The Secret* has been much maligned, as these sorts of
things usually are, and admittedly the focus on material benefit is annoying, but the message hammered home by many
eloquent speakers is that what you focus on gets bigger. So
by focusing on misery and dissatisfaction you get more of it.
Thinking positively takes practice and doesn't come easily
to the melancholy inclined but every time I had a miserable
thought I immediately replaced it with something cheery. I
reminded myself how lucky I was to enjoy good health, to
live in a wonderful flat and have a happy relationship.

I was delighted when within a day of this feverish Pollyanna mental effort I got a call from GMTV inviting me to appear on their breakfast show to discuss my green lifestyle. They wanted to come around to film a sort of green infomercial first, which would be replayed on Lorraine Kelly's morning show the following week.

And so a few days later I welcomed Johnnie, the bouncy GMTV producer, and two cameramen into my flat and prepared to give them my best green spiel. First up I was filmed poking around my worm bin (unfortunately the lid had blown off again and the rain had turned it into a bit of a swamp), then cleaning my windows with vinegar and bits of old newspaper and watering my window boxes with my grubby old bathwater. I energetically scoured pots with lemon and salt and mixed up my bug-zapping vodka and tea tree oil spray which is so useful for sterilising lavatories. I confess I usually get one of my cleaners to do this sort of thing and I had no idea it was so tiring. But a woman's work is never done and the camera crew were hungry for more green insights. Onwards!

Keen to raise awareness of the toxicity of cotton clothes (cotton uses one quarter of the world's pesticides), and to discourage people from buying new undies, I was then filmed rejuvenating my knicker drawer by dying a batch of greying bras and pants bright blue.

'I now have an underwear drawer that is the envy of Elle Macpherson,' I lied waving my strange assortment of mis-shapen undergarments at the camera.

It's actually a very useful tip for revamping one's wardrobe cheaply — buy a tub of cheap dye, pour it into the washing machine with your old greying smalls, and when the wash cycle is finished, hey presto, you have a revamped set of clothes. In theory. If you are keen on the tie-die look anyway.

The *pièce de résistance* had come when I'd somehow persuaded S to be filmed peeing into the compost heap to illustrate the need to save water from excess loo flushing.

'Won't he mind?' asked Johnnie cheerily. 'Mind, what do you mean, mind? He'd love it, all men do,' I explained, warming to my theme. 'It brings out their hunter-gatherer instincts that get reactivated watching those boring Bear Grylls survival-type programmes and that other tedious man who forages in forests and takes hours to make fire from bits of stone.'

But unlike the perky Bear Grylls, S seemed very grumpy when the time came to do his bit for home composting.

'Hurry up!' I told him as he wavered, 'just get on with it!' Which he duly did but only under much sufferance. To be honest, there wasn't much love lost between sulky S and the happy telly guys.

Women are advised not to pee on compost as we are too acidic (there's a surprise), so I was filmed in my bath (full of water blackened with seaweed fertiliser to make it look authentically 'used') to talk about the joys of sharing baths with presumably very grubby friends. Watching the rushes I was concerned that I looked a bit bossy. 'Bossy is good!' joshed Johnnie. 'Brits like bossy. Think of Trinny and Susannah, Kirsty Allsopp and Barbara Woodhouse!' Johnnie didn't look a day over 17; he was far too young to remember Barbara Woodhouse. That's the thing about telly people — they are all so very young, even younger than policemen, to be sure.

But more ignominy was to come. The following week I got

up at the deathly hour of 5 a.m. and arrived at the studio clutching my clanking bag of eco-props. In my bid to turn the cornflake-munching masses green I was weighed down with bicarbonate of soda, bottles of cider vinegar and an interesting looking pair of purple tie-dyed knickers. Coming up in the lift I got talking to the GMTV celebrity divorce expert — she pops in whenever there's a celebrity divorce so, as you can imagine, she's there all the time.

'What's that?' she asked pointing to my drought buster (a hosepipe device which siphons bathwater into your garden).

'Oh,' I replied breezily, 'I'm the new colonic irrigation expert and I'm giving a live demo at 8.30 a.m.' She didn't bat an eyelid, such is the eclectic mix of 'experts' on breakfast telly these days.

My green infomercial was timely as a report had just appeared highlighting the dangers of 'toxic splash' — the four billion chemicals from toiletries and cleaning products flushed into the water systems every day which have a terrible effect on our health, hormone levels, wildlife and which are no doubt implicated in the rise of the dreaded moobs.

After a quick blast of hairspray I was quickly ushered onto Lorraine Kelly's fragrant sofa. I braced myself for some challenging questions about global warming and my homemade cleaning unguents but she seemed more interested in my socialite past when a millennia ago I had enjoyed my short flourishing as an It-girl.

Ancient pictures of me cavorting with long-forgotten C-list celebs were flashed before six million bleary eyes. I squirmed uncomfortably. I had reinvented myself as an eco-worrier and *femme serieuse* — the last thing I wanted was to remind my egalitarian comrades in the Green Party of my posh 'n' purple past. There would be no chance of promotion now surely. But it got worse when the footage was played. Clips of S peeing, me in the black bathwater and then flushing the loo while intoning bossily, 'One third of a householder's water usage is flushed down the loo — what a waste of top-quality drinking water! Remember, if it's brown flush it down; if it's yellow let it mellow.'

Then they replayed the clip of S peeing, just in case anyone had missed it. My goodness he was cross and there were raised voices and smashed pots in the kitchen later that evening. Fortunately Lorraine was very friendly and jolly considering it was only 8.30 a.m., as was everyone else. How do they do it? When do they sleep? I felt I'd aged ten years in one morning. Apparently Nelson Mandela gets up at 4 a.m. every day but he does go to bed at 8.30 p.m. I don't think I could ever manage that.

After my two minutes were up I was shooed off the set by a grinning gofer into the Green Room to collect my stuff. Everyone waved cheerfully and wished me a safe journey home. Grrr. What the hell had they got to be so cheerful about, stuck underground at that time of the morning? They were all so damned chipper I was beginning to feel really depressed. I shuffled off into a waiting taxi clutching my cleaning fluids — I couldn't wait to hand them back to one of my cleaners — and went straight home to bed. Hard work, this telly lark I can tell you. I think I'll stick to the day job. Whatever that is.

Still, television reaches so many more people than newspapers and my infomercial got a good response, mainly emails from eco-minded ladies quite taken with the idea of sending their men outside to pee. 'Maybe he'll never come back in,' remarked one hopefully. Though I was of course

happy to become a poster girl for a mass water-saving movement, I wouldn't want to get one of these well-meaning chaps
into trouble. After all, how can the police tell the difference
between a chap doing his bit for the planet and a flasher?

Chapter 21

Protect me from what I want!

I CONTINUED my feverish positive thinking campaign and, lo and behold, another telly opportunity popped up — this time in the guise of a TV producer called Poppy who had set up a TV company called The Luxury Channel which was making programmes for NBC, the huge American news corporation. It would involve travelling and was just the kind of television break I'd been longing for.

Things started off promisingly. I attended lively meetings in ritzy offices where we all brainstormed ideas for series of green programmes. Green design, green houses, green celebrities (grrr), green travel! Let's take the train to Austria! Switzerland! Tasmania! We'll stay in eco-hotels and film eco-houses! In the bright shiny can-do world of telly everything seemed possible.

Our first day of shooting wasn't a great success. We had decided to find something interesting to film at an eco-trade show at Earls Court. This was a bad idea, as endless solar panel stalls and tarmac firms (these days everyone wants to get on the eco-bandwagon and many stalls at 'eco' fairs are not eco at all) don't make for exciting television. So we hung around for five hours waiting to interview Tim Smitt, founder of the wonderful Eden Project in Cornwall, who was giving a talk.

I was a bit nervous about this to be honest. Despite years of journalism I'd never actually interviewed anybody. I'd been interviewed quite a bit myself, which is very pleasant. I mean what's not to like about someone talking about you for an hour or so and scribbling down every *bon mot* you utter as if it's a pearl of wisdom? But now it was my turn to interview someone I felt a bit at sea. Fortunately Tim has actually done something extremely worthwhile. He set up the Eden Project from scratch and today it is a vast eco-estate comprising of gardens and three enormous pods representing the plant life of different continents. In theory I should have had loads to ask him but boning up on his many press cuttings the night before, I felt increasingly anxious. He'd already been asked everything hundreds of times — it was going to be difficult coming up with something original. He sounded fun though so I thought I could lower the tone and ask him if he was single, but for the rest of the time I must stick to questions about the eco-pods. I felt a renewed admiration for hacks who managed to write readable articles about actors and models who really had nothing interesting to say at all.

During the eco-show Tim gave a very boosting and inspirational talk about building the Eden Project. He strode around gesticulating enthusiastically — with his wild grey mane of untamed hair he reminded me of a caged creature hemmed in by the confines of the stage and he held the audience spellbound. Wow! I thought. But as he left the stage he deflated quite visibly before my eyes. As we made our way to a grubby and dimly lit 'VIP' lounge, I realised with a sinking heart that the audience had had the best of him and I must make do with a tired husk of a man who was exhausted and grumpy.

'Can you speak up?' he snapped as I began on my crum-
pled list of questions. 'I can't hear her at all,' he shouted at
the cameraman as I shuffled my papers nervously. 'She's very
quiet, isn't she?' Honestly, I thought crossly, edging closer,
he must have some sort of tin ear, probably from listening
to deafening pop concerts in the 1960s without wearing ear
plugs — so careless! I didn't dare ask him if he was single; to
be honest I didn't care. Like all the men I'd ever met who
were 'good on paper' he was hard work in the flesh.

I began shouting away at him and to my great relief he was
soon off. He was a great interviewee. But after twenty minutes of it I was getting restive. Conversations really should be
two-way exchanges to have much momentum and I longed to
put up my hand and ask 'Can we talk about me now?' Instead
I waited for Tim to draw breath before looking beseechingly
at the cameraman and saying, 'Fantastic! I think that's it!' I
hope I didn't say, 'That's a wrap!' or anything silly like that
but in my desperation I may have. As the cameraman packed
up he asked Tim respectfully, 'Who would you say is your
eco-hero?' Tim glowered at him. 'Zac Goldsmith?' ventured
the cameraman, coughing nervously. 'GRRR. NO!!' Tim
boomed irritably. 'What about Sienna Miller?' I added mis-
chievously, 'She wears recycled clothes.' But he hadn't heard
me which was probably just as well.

It was no good. Perhaps telly wasn't for me after all — I'd
never be enough of a people person to really enjoy it. I was
amused by the telly insider who exposes the hubris of Telly
Tristans in his anonymous 'Secret Blog of a TV Controller
(aged 33 and ¾)'. In it he writes, 'I remember sitting through
a Channel 4 briefing when Hamish Mykura said he wanted
more programmes that felt like "scaling the north face of
the Eiger". Anyone who is seduced by jargon like this is in
danger of disappearing up their own arse.'

Although I had liked the idea of the universe stripping me of my column in order to create space for these exciting television opportunities, it now seemed a pretty poor exchange. Newspapers were better in every way from the idiotic world of modern TV, with its shallow take on the news, daft reality shows and obsession with trivia and human misery. There is some great TV still being made, but so much of it is dumbed down. Newspapers are obviously hotbeds of trivia and nonsense too but along with Radio 4 they are the last bastion of intelligent reasoned comment. How I missed being part of it all.

But ironically, after years of longing to do telly, offers appeared from all directions. I was frequently invited onto breakfast TV which involved getting up at 4.30 a.m. to talk for two minutes about some eco-related subject (sometimes they even rang at 1 a.m. inviting me in that morning when their preferred guest had presumably cancelled), but what sort of person could possibly be watching television at 6.30 a.m.? A foreign language student once complained that the British people he lodged with set their alarms for 7 a.m. so they could watch breakfast television for two hours before they went to work, so perhaps there really are hordes of people up at the crack of dawn.

Strange requests, like one from an obscure news channel that wanted me to debate why it was better to eat meat than fly if you wanted to reduce your carbon emissions, came winging my way. I had no desire to be a poster girl for eating meat — realistically I would suggest we all cut down on eating meat and flew a lot less. But no, in the brave new world of telly, compromises weren't on.

Donnachadh was surprised that I was rejecting these non-sensical TV 'opportunities'. He said yes to everything on principle as he was very keen to be a green media commentator.

But I didn't think I had the constitution for it after all.

I soldiered on with The Luxury Channel's increasingly unluxurious working methods but morale was fading fast. Despite the swanky offices (probably because of them) remuneration was not forthcoming and people kept disappearing to do properly paid work. One editor decided he'd rather risk his life filming in Iraq than risk not getting paid by Poppy. I only hung on because I didn't have much else to do. But eventually, to my relief, it all fizzled out.

It's interesting that we can spend years yearning for something and then when you get it you realise it doesn't make you happy. I now have a sign on my fridge saying 'Protect me from what I want'; it would save a lot of hassle.

Chapter 22

Festive meltdown

FORTUNATELY it was now Christmas and there was plenty going on, good and bad, to distract me from my grim musings. I really enjoy this time of year — everyone needs an excuse for a party and celebration to light up the long dark nights — though as a 'waste not, want not' green, the massive consumer overdrive does do my head in. I try not to think too much about all the excess packaging, plastic bags, wrapping paper, unwanted gifts and leftover food which contributes to a vast landfill site the size of the Albert Hall being filled every hour. But I live very close to the Albert Hall so just looking at it sets off a terrible Pavlovian response of gloom and unfestive misery.

Scientists get particularly creative around Christmas and band about these eco-doom statistics with great abandon. Someone went to the trouble of working out that the waste created in Britain over Christmas is equivalent to 400,000 double-decker buses, stretching all the way from London to New York City. Not only that but if every family reused just two feet of holiday ribbon, the 38,000 miles of ribbon saved could tie a bow around the entire planet. I like these sorts of statistics because they turn these startling numbers into an amusing and unforgettable visual — I've taken to memorising them as a mental exercise to ward off early Alzheimer's.

In an ideal world we would keep the good bits about Christmas and ditch the hassle, waste and stress involved. Living next door to the Mother Ship, Peter Jones, gives me a ringside seat. Trust me — it can get pretty scary in there in December.

It's a shame that what was once a jolly pagan pageant, lighting up the dreariest darkest days of the year, has turned into this exhausting three-month consumer orgy that leaves us shattered and skint by January. At Christmas our expectations are huge; the festival symbolises the way we'd like our lives to be — loving family and friends, roaring fires, good food, warmth, love and generosity — and how the advertising campaigns exploit this need by brainwashing us into a belief that the more we buy for ourselves and our loved ones, the happier we will be. The reality is that by shopping less we would gain so much more, but who will make money out of telling people that?

Meanwhile, the collapse of religion, traditional Christian precepts and the decline of the family have been replaced with a ravenous materialism and an escalation of festive fanaticism. We have replaced our Christian God with a shiny new material god; the Argos catalogue has replaced the Bible, but it's a pretty poor substitute. This new god is far more demanding than the Christian one who was happy with a weekly appearance at church and a few kind thoughts. His replacement demands 24/7 attention and needs to be fed with an endless supply of unnecessary and planet-destroying possessions. Yet despite our increasing disregard for Christian principles we still have spiritual yearnings which aren't being satisfied, hence the rise in spiritual shopping

— which ironically is often the most expensive shopping of all.

I can't help but notice that while most of the women in festive meltdown (and it is only women) look and sound just like me — even down to the precise shade of Harbour Club blonde — I am not of them at all. This is because I am in fact a man. Despite having a poor sense of direction, no interest in gadgets or football and not looking like a man, nonetheless I am, most definitely, a man. Women all fall into three categories: men, women and girls. Men fall into three categories: men, boys and hairdressers. It sounds simplistic but spookily enough you'll find no trouble fitting practically everyone you know into one of these compartments once you give it a go.

One of my principal man characteristics is that I celebrate Christmas like a man — that is, I do nothing very much at all. Men create far fewer carbon emissions than women at this time of year, as all most of them do is hide from their snapping turtle womenfolk in sheds or slump in front of the telly, which as long as they switch it off at the mains when they turn in, is far more eco-friendly than driving around buying their share of the estimated sixty-five million unwanted, over-packaged presents and forests of wrapping paper (enough to stretch all around Guernsey according to another eco-statistician) with which to wrap them in. Women need to become more like men at Christmas, which will reduce their stress levels hugely.

I can't understand why so many of my girlfriends buy presents for everyone they've ever known; the resulting hassle means they have to be practically hospitalised for stress by December 25. One buys gifts — things like trays and tapestry kits — for her cleaner, her facialist and her hairdresser.

Letting go of the Glitz

My hairdresser doesn't want a present; he wants a nice big tip. Like Julia Roberts in *Pretty Woman* he insists that 'cash works for me'. This is not considered to be very thoughtful, but who wants thoughts when you could have money? I'm sorry but am I missing something here? Last year a friend ambushed me just before Christmas with a compilation book of Jeremy Clarkson's columns and Victoria Beckham's *Style Secrets*. It is said it's the thought that counts, but these sorts of thoughts are of no use to anyone.

You'd think being so fussy about presents I'd be a very thoughtful buyer, but I'm just as bad. Inspired by my favourite Neanderthal sex god, DCI Gene Hunt from the cult TV series set in the 1970s, *Life on Mars*, who stalks the streets of crime wearing big collars, clip-on kipper ties and foot-long sideburns, I bought S an excitingly retro 1970s green shirt with definite three-day-week appeal. The outfit was complemented with a pair of bright green hemp boxer shorts I bought at an eco-show. They're the sort of thing Kermit the Frog might wear — if he were a man, not a frog — and they disappeared soon afterwards.

The thing is that if Christmas was left to men you'd end up with a tree and massive amounts of booze. They are happily free of the need to send cards, buy fairy lights or stay up till midnight making mince pies. It's time for 'we women' (as they say in the *Daily Mail*) to drop our festive expectations and embrace a seasonal slow-down — for the sake of our sanity as well as the planet's.

As a man, buying the Christmas tree is, of course, my big must-do, even though it is an eco-conundrum. In theory, buying a tree should be a good thing but most Christmas trees are grown in vast mono-plantations and drenched in pesticides. While they will soak up some CO_2 these forests are eerie places with very little biodiversity. Cutting down such a tree, transporting it hundreds of miles, draping electric lights over it, then discarding it three weeks later is such a waste. A better option, especially if you have a garden, is to buy a British one which has roots so it can be replanted in the garden afterwards. I did this one year and my tree died anyway, but this was probably because my rooftop patio is probably not the best place to plant a Norway spruce — in a garden it would have stood a good chance. A staggering six million fir trees are bought in the UK at Christmas, many of which end up in landfill, unless you are lucky enough to have a council that will collect them to grind down as mulch — a far better solution.

Donnachadh has a dream of creating a Christmas forest. If some of the six million people who buy a fir tree bought a different type of tree (bay and holly trees can look very festive when they're decorated), kept their thermostat turned down a few notches so it doesn't bake to death and then planted it outside after Christmas, we'd create beautiful lasting swathes of green throughout the country.

Last year, keen not to kill another fir tree, I splashed out on a holly bush, which I decorated with old ribbons, paste jewellery, bunches of cinnamon sticks, strings of fake pearls and fir cones. It looked very attractive over Christmas but like my fir tree, promptly died as soon as I put it outside on the patio. Its dried up remains are still on my roof waiting to go in the wood-burning stove, so at least it will provide us with fuel and won't be landfilled.

Observing the festive panic makes me feel a certain amount of *schadenfreude* and is one of the reasons I like Christmas so much. Childless women like me are often portrayed as sad and lonely spinsters at this time of year, wishing we could swap our empty lives with those of busy mothers who are considered properly fulfilled, racing around caring for their husbands and children. But observing the modern mother I just feel hugely relieved I don't have their mountain of obligations — I can't sit through a sell-out show in the West End without wanting to boil my own head, so how on earth would I manage to sit through a school play or sports day? Yes, I may end up a lonely old bag with no children to visit me in the old people's home, but I'll face that when the time comes.

As it is I have very little to do in the festive season. I have two proper presents to buy, one for S and one for my mother. Fortunately the latter is of a similar mindset to me and does not crave any more things but hopes for something small and useful — a space-clearing room spray from the renowned homeopaths Ainsworths went down very well, as did a jar of grilled aubergine slices marinated in herbs and good olive oil. I keep a bottom drawer with quickie gifts — lovely handmade lavender bags from the farmers' market and some of the less appealing scented candles I'm presented with for immediate regifting should someone drop round with an unexpected present that must be reciprocated, but that's it.

Making a conscious decision to opt out of the hassle stops one becoming stressed-out and more able to appreciate what Christmas is all about. In theory anyway. One of the more successful birthday presents (from his point of view) I gave to S were tickets to an Arsenal match. Truly no good deed goes unpunished. How can I ever forget the misery of the piercing Siberian wind whistling through my organic thermal underwear? Football is safer than it was in the bad old thuggish days but there are still many other dangers. Being out of sync with the general mood (I was reading *Hello!* for most of the match) meant whenever there was a goal I nearly got my jaw dislocated by a great surge of muscly men leaping up around me — it's a miracle I wasn't disembowelled. S was no use, having suddenly morphed into a tribal warlike creature singing songs and waving his arms around in an alarming manner — rather like Donnachadh's wind turbine during a storm.

Taking your loved ones to the theatre is another popular eco-friendly zero-waste present idea — if you like drama that is. Not being a culture-vulture, tickets to the theatre fill me with gloom — plays go on far too long while the interval is too short. You're enjoying a drink and a spot of people-gazing and then some terrible deafening bell is rung summoning you to your grubby, miniscule, velour seat where you remain trapped for an inestimable time. S once dragged me under sufferance to the fashionable Almeida Theatre in Islington where they have replaced the tiny filthy seats with trendy long benches. But all this means is that fatties spread out over three seats worth of space leaving the rest of us even more scrunched up than before.

I got to appreciate intervals properly after the 2001 election when I stood as the Green Party candidate in Chelsea against Michael Portillo. During the count, my small band of supporters were briefly rebooted when Mr Portillo plonked himself down at our table to say hello before quickly rushing off to meet friends at the theatre — not for the play but for a drink in the interval. Perhaps theatres should start selling interval tickets — they could bolster the occasion with interesting cocktails and highlights of the play in question on a revolving loop. Then busy culture-vultures could get their fix and still be able to join in arty discussions with their intellectual friends at Islington dinner parties afterwards.

As you might imagine I don't get many presents — no one dares take the risk and now S just buys me stuff he wants himself. The most expensive presents he's given me, a camcorder and a DVD player, were so complicated I gave them back to him, which was the perfect solution, as I knew he secretly wanted them anyway. A vibrator was another unsuccessful present which with its enormous girth and terrible reverberating spikes and lumps looked agonising. Anyone who has ever suffered from cystitis would quite naturally run a mile from such an instrument of torture. 'But ten million women have bought one,' he insisted, but I reckon it is men who are buying them because of their insidious belief that technology is the solution to everything — including global warming.

The other thing I don't like about vibrators is that surely they must desensitize one from the real thing, rather like putting chilli pepper on all your meals; after a while you stop being able to taste food that hasn't been wildly over seasoned. But even I couldn't think of anything to do with an unpacked vibrator (I hadn't used it but how could anyone prove this?) and so it languishes in S's shed beneath years worth of unwanted gadgets and broken electrical equipment.

After being given the vibrator I'd gone to the trouble of writing 'Julia does not want gadgets' and Sellotaped it to the vodka bottle in the deep freeze where S could not miss it. I had to do this as my previous 'no gadget entreaties' had fallen on deaf ears because, as experts insist, men are not wired to hear women (although you don't need to be an expert to know that). I thought I was getting through when he announced he was going to buy me some green underwear he'd seen 'in a dream'. You can never have too many green undergarments so I waited in anticipation that my grey sagging stocks might soon be replaced. Sadly the garments proffered weren't green but an unappetising purple, so no good. If you are given unwearable underwear don't chuck it into landfill and contribute to the methane problem; if you can't return them to the shop (the obvious solution but sometimes it takes one wearing before you realise you don't like something and then it's too late), many charity shops and textile recycling banks will take bags of clean unsaleable clothes and rags to mince up into low-grade furniture stuffing — so if it's not good enough to wear on your bum it can end up under it. Failing that you could dye them in the washing machine.

There is a lot of emphasis at this time of year from fashion writers on finding the perfect Christmas dress to wear to festive shindigs. But as writer A. A. Gill points out, if you don't put on any weight you will never need to buy any new clothes anyway. I don't get much opportunity to wear the lovely dresses I bought years ago at the height of It-girldoom, so why would I need any more? And who on earth cares if one wears the same dress again and again? It's so much work to find something one loves — why not wear it as much as possible? But then, I am a man, so the concept of a new dress for each outing is something I can't comprehend.

But unfortunately the government doesn't want us to shop less, while the media colludes by avidly reporting whether retailers are having a 'good' or 'bad' Christmas and uses this as a yardstick with which to judge the general well-being and success of the nation. More shopping equals more GDP (gross domestic product), but this has nothing to do with gross national happiness, the real arbiter of our contentment.

William Leith castigates consumerism in his two depressing but utterly readable novels, *The Hungry Years* and *Bits of Me Are Falling Apart*. 'Everything is a commodity,' he writes in the latter:

Just look at, God, I don't know, anything. Like body hair, women used to shave their legs and armpits and pluck their eyebrows and get their hair cut. Now they wax their legs and shave their armpits and trim their pubic hair and wax their pubic hair and dye their eyelashes and tint their hair simultaneously with several colours and supplement it with hair extensions, and every new activity requires tools and materials, such as trimming devices and depilatory creams and laser hair-removal machines. Now men are waxing their chests, and soon they'll be shaping and trimming their pubic hair. It's economic growth. It's unstoppable.

And now retailers are hiring experts to advise them on how to sell more stuff, experts who cheerfully tell us that, if it wasn't for impulse purchasing, if it wasn't for people buying stuff that they don't strictly need, or even want, 'the economy would collapse'.

Speaking from experience, the best present I ever received didn't cost a penny, resulted in zero carbon emissions and brought me more happiness than anything I could have bought. I had fallen out with a close relative but instead of talking it over face to face, this resentment festered over time making me more disappointed and unhappy. So just before Christmas, seduced by festive spirit, I decided to drop my grudge and arranged to meet him for lunch. Within half an hour I'd got everything off my chest, we'd chatted and laughed and all umbrages had melted into thin air. A load had lifted from my shoulders and I left feeling lighter and brighter. It was the best present I could have given myself. It didn't do much for the economy; the treasury were not celebrating as no baubles had been bought, but it did a lot for two people's gross national happiness.

Sometimes the hardest but most valuable thing we can do at Christmas is to create peace at home, with our families, friends and neighbours. Creating peace here is the start for creating peace everywhere. From Buddhism I've learnt the importance of creating harmony in the microcosm because this makes peace in the macrocosm possible — after all, how can we expect the Israelis and Palestinians or the Chinese and Tibetans to live in harmony if we can't live in harmony with our families and those closest to us? Looking at the world this way makes peace our responsibility and not just the duty of governments.

I speak from experience, as for many years I had a difficult relationship with my family and it's taken some effort from us all to get things onto an even, happier keel. I really credit my Buddhist practice with this, as it has made me more reflecting, patient and able to see things from another perspective. Without it I would have remained a grudge-bearing, unforgiving creature for sure. But some years ago relations were so bad I had nowhere to spend Christmas day so I decided to spend it doing charity work. Nichiren Daishonin wrote in the thirteenth century: 'If you light a lantern for another, it will also lighten your own way,' which made me hope that helping others might cheer me up a bit too. But the homeless charity to which I volunteered my services put me on a waiting list, as they were deluged with offers of help. It made me wonder if, like me, perhaps some of these souls were looking for an acceptable way of escaping their family obligations.

Sometimes it's much easier to make allowances for those we don't know than those we do. And it's ironic that for 363 days a year charities are crying out for help but on those two days they have to turn it away. Still, it is a laudable thing to do, whatever one's motivation.

In the final reckoning, my best Christmas was one of the simplest and the quietest. S and I were quite alone — we battened down the hatches, danced to the Bee Gees, watched *Dad's Army* (eagerly pointing out sightings of spivvy Walker, who makes me laugh because he reminds me of S), feasted on roast chicken and toasted our amazing survival as a couple with a bottle of pink fizz (for me) and organic beers (for him). No rows, no rellos and no gadgets. Heaven.

Chapter 23

What's the point?

I KNOW people sometimes ask what's the point of me doing anything when the Chinese are building three coal-fired stations a week and carbon emissions are continuing to rise globally as the developing world wants to experience the gas-guzzling delights of electricity, fast cars and cheap air travel (well, delight and cheap air travel is a bit of an oxymoron but you get the picture).

But it is worth doing your bit to make a difference. Small actions have huge effects — if most people in the UK turned off their standby appliances at night we could close three nuclear power stations.

And even if the UK population's private habits account for only a tiny percentage of the problem we can't ask China and India to reduce their carbon emissions unless we lead the way ourselves. And surely it's better to ease ourselves into a sustainable lifestyle now than wait for the government to enforce carbon rationing, which looks increasingly likely.

But talk is cheap and action is thin on the ground. The phrase 'green fatigue' has been coined to express the inertia of those who are apparently overwhelmed by the environmental crisis. But I think this apathy is just an excuse for those who can't be bothered anyway. The truth is that when we take action we become engaged with the problem and energised and uplifted by doing something, no matter how small, about it. We have created these problems and equally we have the ingenuity to solve them.

Geothermal boreholes that harness the warmth of the earth to provide us with power, bugs that gobble up plastic so that it doesn't pollute landfill sites, planes powered by algae and solar-powered cargo ships are just some of the exciting new technologies that are being developed. But although technological solutions are necessary to dig ourselves out of the problem, nothing will change unless humanity makes a conscious shift away from greed and believing that material benefits are the path to happiness. The trouble is our entire culture is based on the myth that the more we buy the happier we become.

The King of Bhutan suggests that GNH (gross national happiness), not GNP (gross national product) should be the true arbiter of a nation's contentment. After all, if you think back to your happiest time it's usually not buying a house or a new car but something far more prosaic like falling in love, the birth of a child or satisfaction for work well done. One of my happiest moments came when I was travelling back from four days in Faliraki where I'd been sent on my first assignment by the *Daily Mail*. My editor called to say the big chief, Paul Dacre, loved the article I'd just filed (this has never happened before or since), but I danced in the aisles of the train at the unaccustomed praise.

The threat facing our world often seems nebulous and far away. In some circles it is still fashionable to decry global warming, claiming it's part of a natural cycle and nothing to do with the extraordinary pressures humans are putting on the planet. I was shocked in Switzerland when a bunch of stonkingly rich parents and children educated at swanky Le Rosey all poured cold water on Al Gore and boasted at having resisted showing *An Inconvenient Truth* at the school because it was 'propaganda' — because Gore travelled on planes apparently his message could be utterly discounted. In addition, to believe in his message would imply criticism of their own wasteful lifestyles — the houses, the cars and the planes would make them feel unconscionably guilty. It reminded me a bit of a disparaging TV researcher going around Donnachadh's house and expressing great disapproval when she saw that he had an (extremely small) fridge. 'I've got a fridge because I have to eat and don't want my food to go off! Besides,' he pointed out exasperatedly, 'to be carbon neutral I'd have to stop breathing!'

With rich Westerners burying their heads in the sand and doing the equivalent of dancing on the Titanic, for those on the front line with no influence — the poor in Bangladesh, the inhabitants of the islands of Tuvalu which are already sinking beneath the waves and the Inuits in Greenland — the situation is depressing. But it's not too late to take action; action will inspire and invigorate us. As Gandhi said, 'Almost everything we do will seem insignificant but it is important that you do it.'

Sometimes an event or experience can trigger a change in one's thinking. At least it did for me. A photo and a sprig of jasmine recently fell out of an old novel during a clean out and brought memories flooding back of a hot, sunny summer in the South of France which altered the way I thought about everything, forever.

One sweltering May, Jane invited me to Cannes. We were in our mid-thirties and this trip was, in retrospect, the last gasp of It-girl-doom. We could just about still get away with being skittish and girlish; a year later it would have been too late. That terrible phrase, 'she was like an exquisite plate of food left out overnight' was on the verge of applying to us, but not quite …

We stayed with one of Jane's billionaire ex-boyfriends, Nico Pollatino, with whom she had remained on friendly terms. Nico lived in a palatial villa on the Cote d'Azur which was a beacon to the famous. Mick Jagger, Elle Macpherson, George Clooney and any number of gorgeous supermodels, hedge fund tycoons and Hollywood actors were to be found lounging beside the infinity pool in the blazing sunshine sipping freshly squeezed tropical fruit juices or champagne. Everybody was in high spirits (or appeared to be), but like a round peg in a square hole I felt nervous and uncomfortable. Being unhappy in paradise magnifies your misery — what excuse could I possibly have for being miserable? I was with the cool gang! But it was absolutely exhausting keeping up with the sophisticated small talk, changes of clothes, extreme glamour, success and physical perfection of everyone we met.

Every other day Jane and I would hot foot it along to the Hotel du Cap in Antibes in her tiny hired Fiat Panda. Liveried flunkeys would grandly take her car keys and park it round the back next to Bentleys, Rolls and Lamborghinis. Not the place you want to park if you have status anxiety! Once installed by the vast sun-drenched open-air pool, Nico's business contacts and Eurotrash friends of Jane's would ply us with the hotel's signature champagne and strawberry juice cocktails — at thirty euros a pop these don't come cheap, but marvellously we had entered a parallel universe where women (provided they are young and pretty enough) don't pay for a thing. Having always paid my own way I did think this was one aspect of this life I could get used to!

What's the point?

The Hotel du Cap is a legend and in the most lovely position, jutting out on rocks overlooking a stunning expanse of azure ocean. The staff are famously grumpy and you can't use credit cards — you must pay in cash — but this stroppiness only adds to the otherworldly allure of the place. It is also where my grandparents spent their honeymoon in the late 1930s, and it hasn't changed much since then.

One evening Nico took us all to the *Vanity Fair* party at the hotel, the hottest ticket in town and practically impossible to get into. As we arrived, queues of desperate would-be guests begging the bad-tempered concierges to let them in were being turned away because they weren't on the magical list. But thanks to the awesome clout of Nico, that week Jane and I had access all areas. And what an evening it was! The white turreted hotel gleamed in the moonlight, cicadas chirped and the sea whooshed beyond the jasmine-scented lawns. Gorgeous actresses shimmied across the shining parquet floors draped in stunning dresses, and handsome men, nut brown from schmoozing in the sun, clinked glasses and flirted and fell in and out of love. It was like a movie set come to life.

But all was not quite perfect in paradise. An acquaintance from London was spotted sobbing in a corner because her boyfriend was flirting uncontrollably with Uma Thurman. Like me, she was worn out with the efforts of schmoozing night and day and, unable to distract her boyfriend, she soon left in tears. But emboldened by champagne and so many beautiful people I was on cloud nine. Jane was soon whisked off by a handsome Argentinian billionaire who had witnessed her stylish diving earlier in the day — she can do somersaults, back flips, you name it — and began to woo her with protestations of undying love. But this is quite normal at the Hotel du Cap — people fall madly in love for an evening and then it wears off. Maybe they put something in the cock-tails. Or maybe it is the magic of Antibes ...

While Jane was frolicking with the South American steel magnate I was adopted by a well-connected Monégasque lesbian who knew everyone. 'I'll introduce you to Prince Albert,' she hissed, collaring him as he wandered past followed by a stream of Amazonian Victoria's Secret models. 'Hey, your Serene Highness, meet Julia Stephenson.' I must have been completely sozzled by then because I gave him my card and told him, 'If you're ever in London and would like someone to show you around, do give me a ring.' He was very polite and took the card and put it into his breast pocket. Needless to say I never got a call. Thus emboldened I bounced up to the *soigné* James Fox by the bar and said how much I had enjoyed his classic film, *The Servant*.

Then the Monacan lesbian reappeared and introduced me to a desperately handsome, tall, dark, moody man knocking back cocktails by himself in the corner. He reminded me of the dark, dishy Mr Big from *Sex in the City*, so how ironic that he was Candace Bushnell's then boyfriend who was consoling himself as she was away finishing a book. Now, she is beautiful, bright and witty, and you'd think he wouldn't have eyes for anyone else, but we hit it off immediately. The chemistry sizzled, more cocktails were consumed, we chatted away and then suddenly he took me in his arms and pulled me out onto the moonlit terrace where we snogged for hours. Really you can't leave a chap alone for five minutes!

'You're adorable,' he kept whispering tantalisingly and we snogged some more. 'Come back to my villa, I'm flying home first thing in the morning ...'

I was very tempted but amazingly resisted invitations to his villa (not being able to sleep without my sleep mask and ear plugs was probably the reason, not anything more moral

What's the point?

I'm afraid to say — lack of spontaneity has certainly kept the notches on my bedpost down to fairly manageable levels) and hitched a ride back to base with Jane who had similarly extracted herself from the Argentinian steel magnate, who had by then promised her the sky, the stars and all his tin mines in Patagonia.

The next day we went back to the Hotel du Cap so Jane could reconvene with her oleaginous Latino. I was feeling horribly crushed. Mr Big had returned to London — and the lovely Candace — and had not called, despite begging me for my number, and Jane's tin man gave her the cold shoulder and had taken up just as suddenly with one of the Victoria's Secret models. The euphoria of the previous evening had dissipated like a puff of smoke and we were back in the cruel and cold real world.

It was time to go home.

After this, something in me changed and I gave up chasing a dream of what I thought life should be like and became happier with what I had. I stopped going out for the sake of it, had a big clear out, gave away a lot of clothes, lost touch with a lot of people and was finally *bien dans ma peau.* It was time to live a simpler life.

I know we live in a youth-worshipping culture, but the terrible thing about being young (or youngish) are all the efforts one is often compelled to make to fit in. Now I'm in my forties I think, what the hell? I'm just going to do what I like. But up to that point I was searching for a Shangri-La that was always just beyond my reach. These days Shangri-La is staying in and watching *Desperate Housewives* or going out to the movies, and I get just as much of a buzz from altering my old clothes than buying new ones, but for many years I wanted more, more,

more. Many dreary things come with age but there are huge compensations too.

My father says that when he was young, people were happier because they couldn't compare themselves with other people so much, as without television and the media no one knew how other people lived. In his seminal book, *Affluenza,* Oliver James writes:

> *relentless exposure to images of wealth and beauty spill over and poison lives beyond the sitting room. Since programmes are saturated with exceptionally attractive people living abnormally opulent lives, expectations of what is 'normal' are raised — and every few minutes come the advertisements ... Once, we used to keep up with Joneses who lived in our street. Now, thanks largely to TV, it's the Beckhams. In 1950, people read in the newspapers about the royal family, the aristocracy and film stars ... but it never occurred to them that these people were anything like them or that they could ever live those kinds of lives.*

But today, as we are bombarded with the glamorous lives of celebrities and the wealthy on the internet, magazines and television, their unsustainable lives have become the blueprint to which the majority of us aspire.

My week with the zillionaires in Cannes offered me a glimpse of the world which so many dream of inhabiting. It's a world where everything is judged on skin deep beauty, the size of your boat, your boobs and your bank balance. You have to have a thick skin and a steely ambition to survive. I'm so glad I experienced this world because I had to live through it to see it for what it was.

It's a cliché, but happiness comes from the inside. Take Mr Big at Cannes. He was handsome, rich, eligible and successful. But he was a flirt and a banker who made his fortune by moving bits of money around and creating nothing very memorable. When I bumped into him a year later at a party I wondered what on earth I'd seen in him. A man like that was good on paper, if you go for that kind of thing, but not right for me. Yet I spent most of my youth dreaming of that sort of man, and the lifestyle that went with it, so no wonder I was so unsatisfied.

While I was no more compulsive than many others I was definitely, looking back, on a rather pointless treadmill, trying to get somewhere that was just out of reach. I'm not smug enough to think I've reached the pot of gold at the end of the rainbow, but living a simpler life with more honest values has made me much more content.

Giving up on the sweat of trying to achieve things that didn't make me happy — like 'making it' in television — gives me more time to do the things that I really enjoy, like pottering around the house, reading, cooking, lying around in fields, or when no fields are available, in the recently installed hammock on my roof.

Shrinking our carbon emissions and leaving the ancient sunlight (i.e. coal) in the ground where it belongs is a by-product of living a happier life. We gain, and so does the planet. Today I sit at my desk and dream of the past and wonder at how much I've changed. The theory that we replace our entire body every seven years is perhaps one explanation of how my craving for the gas-guzzling high life was replaced by a yearning for a quieter, happier, more satisfying existence. Maybe the next seven years will change me back again, but I hope not!

Epilogue

As A final postscript I must recount something that happened during the final editing of this book.

Whilst running down the King's Road, not looking where I was going, I tripped in a pot-hole and fell, splat on my face in the street. My ankle was sore and twisted and I could hardly walk the short distance home. The next day, when it was still no better I limped off to A&E where I was firmly strapped into a surgical boot. At least, I consoled myself, I had avoided having a plaster cast fitted. However, as a spiritual shopper (in recovery) I knew this experience must have happened to *teach* me something, but what exactly?

A few days later I went for my first appointment with the orthopaedic surgeon. I presumed he'd take another X-ray, tell me to take it easy and that would be it. But to my horror, he looked at the X-ray, insisted it was fractured badly and that I must have a plaster cast fitted straight away. As I hobbled home, facing up to a fortnight of very limited movement and the grim prospect of my plaster-imprisoned foot becoming grubbier, sweatier and itchier by the day, I was relieved to find S already back from work and making one of his vile signature dishes in the kitchen. For once I held my tongue (forty minutes to chop a carrot!) and we shuffled into the sitting room, him with a beer and me with a consoling glass of non-dose Laurent Perrier champagne (non-dose means no sugar is added during fermentation; now I could barely walk I needed to cut cals wherever possible).

As we sat ruminating in the darkness I wondered if he'd ever thought about getting married and why on earth hadn't he asked me yet. To be honest, every time we had raised the 'M' word I'd dismissed it, as the thought of being responsible for anyone's debts was an alarming thought (in my naivety I hadn't given this issue a moment's thought when I married the first time round). Why would anyone marry, I had since reasoned, when the whole shebang was riskier than Lloyd's of London? But that didn't mean I didn't want to be asked. Marriage is a gamble but there is something undeniably romantic and ridiculously optimistic about telling the world that *this* is the person I'm going to spend the rest of my life with. Besides, I really wanted a new name; I was still using my ex-husband's name because I hadn't been able to face the hassle involved in changing it back again. Now, with features editors hardly mowing me down with requests for articles, I had plenty of time to engage in this bureaucratic name-changing nightmare.

And so, sitting in the dark, emboldened by fizz, I quietly asked, 'Have you ever thought that we might get married?'

He looked surprised, 'I hadn't really thought about it …' And then he was silent for a moment. 'I didn't really think you were up for it … but why don't we – let's do it!' And carried away by excitement he jumped to his feet then fell onto a bended knee and looked into my eyes, 'Will you marry me?'

'Of course!' I replied happily, relieved that he hadn't batted the crazy idea completely out of court.

Epilogue

In the euphoria of the moment he jumped up, knocking over my champagne glass which smashed into a thousand pieces. It had been the final remaining glass of a set given to my parents for their wedding, and despite the misery of their relationship I had treasured it. Breaking it, I felt, was either a sign we were doing the right thing, or perhaps, a terrible warning. It was in any case a dramatic sign which I chose to see as a positive breaking with the past and old family miseries. It symbolised a clean slate.

Saying that, we have no desire to rush into marriage (we've set the date provisionally for November 2025), as being engaged is a delightful and under-appreciated state in itself, signifying love and commitment without any ghastly legal obligations. Besides, we still haven't started on the building work yet, which must remain the great test of any relationship — if we can survive that we can surely survive anything.

But just having the marriage discussion, and both realising we felt the same way, has brought a security and a depth to our relationship. I like knowing that we both love each other so much that we won't both bolt at the first sign of a big row. That we'll stick it out through the good and bad times. That we are saying to ourselves and the world, this is it, we're off the market, we're a team till the end.

Isn't it wonderful in this logical, scientific, godless age that the majority of people are prepared at some stage in their lives to jump off the precipice, throw caution to the wind, ignore the terrible risk of losing their house, savings, worldly goods, potential children and sanity in the very real threat of divorce and, against the odds, say 'I do', all for one special person. It's utterly irrational and completely wonderful what we will risk for love.

I hope my story will be an inspiration to others. If the credit crunch can teach us anything it is to value what really matters and encourage us to look beyond a person's status, car, bank balance, house or lifestyle and appreciate what lies beneath. At one time I thought a wealthy Porsche-driving Saville Row-suited plutocrat was the answer to my romantic dreams. How wrong I was and how lucky that I followed my heart, not my head, and ended up with the diametric opposite.

Buddhist sage Nichiren Daishonin summed it up thus: 'More valuable than treasures in a storehouse are the treasures of the body, and the treasures of the heart are the most valuable of all.'

About the author

JULIA STEPHENSON lives in Chelsea where she works inconsistently as a freelance writer whilst supervising the conversion of her roof top eyrie into the first carbon neutral property in Sloane Square. Helped and hindered by her boyfriend, fortuitously a builder, and five of his super-handy brothers similarly employed in the building trade, she is fully occupied making cups of tea, soaking old newspapers in the bath to make briquettes for the wood-burning stove, fretting about the efficacy of domestic wind turbines and hoping the builders don't smoke the hemp bricks before they lay them. The work has been going on some time now. During her free time she can be found in the recovery position. She is the author of *Pandora's Diamond* and *Chalet Tiara*.